Soviet Policies Toward the Nordic Countries

Soviet Policies Toward the Nordic Countries

ÖRJAN BERNER

UNIVERSITY PRESS OF AMERCA
LANHAM•NEW YORK•LONDON

**THE CENTER FOR
INTERNATIONAL AFFAIRS
HARVARD UNIVERSITY**

Copyright © 1986 by
the President and Fellows of Harvard College

University Press of America,® Inc.

4720 Boston Way
Lanham, MD 20706

3 Henrietta Street
London WC2E 8LU England

Printed in the United States of America

Library of Congress Cataloging in Publication Data

Berner, Örjan, 1937-
    Soviet policies toward the Nordic countries.

    Shorter version published under title: Sovjet &
Norden. © 1985.
    Bibliography: p.
    1. Scandinavia—Military relations—Soviet Union.
2. Finland—Military relations—Soviet Union.
3. Soviet Union—Military relations—Scandinavia.
4. Soviet Union—Military relations—Finland.   I. Title.
UA646.7.B4713   1986   327.47048   86-9087
ISBN 0-8191-5381-8 (alk. paper)
ISBN 0-8191-5382-6 (pbk. : alk. paper)

Spaceship Earth and Dymaxian Sky–Ocean Map
Copyright 1954, 1984 Buckminster Fuller Institute

The Dymaxian Sky–Ocean Map used on the cover of this book
was invented by Buckminster Fuller. The map shows our planet
without any visible distortion of the relative shape and sizes
of the land and sea areas and without any breaks in the continental contours.

For additional information about the map, contact
the Buckminster Fuller Institute
1743 South La Cienega Boulevard
Los Angeles, California 90035
(213) 837-7710

Co-published by arrangement with the
Center for International Affairs, Harvard University

The Center for International Affairs provides a forum for the
expression of responsible views. It does not necessarily agree with those views.

All University Press of America books are produced on acid-free
paper which exceeds the minimum standards set by the
National Historical Publications and Records Commission.

The Center for International Affairs Executive Committee, 1985-86

Samuel P. Huntington, *Eaton Professor of the Science of Government; Director, Center for International Affairs*

Leslie H. Brown, *Director of the Fellows Program*

Richard N. Cooper, *Maurits C. Boas Professor of International Economics*

Jill Crystal, *Ph.D. Candidate in Government*

Stephan Haggard, *Assistant Professor of Government*

Chester D. Haskell, *Executive Officer*

Stanley Hoffmann, *C. Douglas Dillon Professor of the Civilization of France; Chairman, Center for European Studies*

Herbert Kelman, *Richard Clarke Cabot Professor of Social Ethics*

Robert O. Keohane, *Professor of Government*

Joseph S. Nye, Jr., *Professor of Government; Director, Center for Science and International Affairs*

Dwight H. Perkins, *Harold Hitchings Burbank Professor of Political Economy; Director, Harvard Institute for International Development*

Robert D. Putnam, *Professor of Government; Chairman, Department of Government*

Henry Rosovsky, *Lewis P. and Linda L. Geyser University Professor*

Sidney Verba, *Carl H. Pforzheimer University Professor; Director of the University Library*

Ezra Vogel, *Professor of Sociology*

The Center for International Affairs is an autonomous multidisciplinary research institution within Harvard University's Faculty of Arts and Sciences. Founded in 1958, the Center seeks to provide a stimulating environment for a diverse group of scholars and practitioners studying various aspects of international affairs. Its purpose is the development and dissemination of knowledge concerning the essential features and crucial trends of international relations. Major Center research programs include national security affairs, U.S. relations with Europe, Japan, Africa, and other areas of the world, nonviolent sanctions in conflict and defense, international economic policy, and other critical issues. At any given time, over 160 individuals are working at the Center, including faculty members from Harvard and neighboring institutions, practitioners of international affairs, visiting scholars, research associates, postdoctoral fellows, and graduate and undergraduate student associates.

To Benedicte, Axel, and Mikael

CONTENTS

About the Author

Orjan Berner was born in 1937 in Lund, Sweden. After studies at Lund University and Stockholm University (LL.B. and M.A.), he joined the Swedish Foreign Ministry in 1960. He served in New York at the Swedish Mission to the United Nations in 1961-64, in Stockholm at the Foreign Ministry, and later as Assistant Director of SIPRI (Stockholm International Peace Research Institute) in 1964-67. He was posted to the Swedish embassies in Peking in 1967-70 and in Moscow in 1970-74, and was then appointed head of the Foreign Ministry's Department of International Organizations, a post he held until 1978 when he was appointed Minister of the Swedish Embassy in Paris. In 1983-84, he spent a sabbatical year at the Center for International Affairs, Harvard University. Since November 1984, he has been the Swedish Ambassador to Poland. His previous publications include various smaller studies and articles on international organizations and foreign relations, and a book entitled *Kristin Svensson* (1981).

PREFACE

This book is the product of a sabbatical year spent at the Center for International Affairs at Harvard University in 1983-84. Neither the Swedish government, which I normally serve as a diplomat, nor any other official body is in any way responsible for the views expressed in this text. They are my own. The facts, as can be seen, are gathered entirely from sources open to the public.

The book is a survey of a long period covering several countries. Scarcity of time and space in itself would prevent any claims to originality or profundity on such a large subject. My sources are principally Soviet media, but I have also relied heavily on the considerable Nordic and Western literature available on Soviet dealings with individual Nordic countries. There is not much written on the broader subject of Nordic-Soviet relations. The close ties between the Nordic countries, the interlocking foreign and security policies of these states, and the Soviet propensity to view the whole area as a loose grouping provide good reasons for such a perspective.

I have singled out a few simple principles in Soviet policy making toward the Nordic group, but I do not try to construct any grand theories to describe this behavior simply because I am unable to do so and suspect that any effort of this kind would be fairly fruitless. The story, so to say, speaks for itself.

Many friends and colleagues at Harvard and in Stockholm have read the manuscript and made suggestions. My thanks go to them as well as to the Fellows Program of the Center for International Affairs and its splendid staff, all of them close friends who have given much help. I am likewise in intellectual debt to other colleagues at the CFIA and at the Russian

Research Center, whose solid expertise on Soviet matters I had occasion to admire. Special thanks go to my editor, Anne Fitzpatrick.

A shorter version of this book was published in Sweden in January 1985.

Orjan Berner

INTRODUCTION

Soviet policies toward the five states in the neighboring Nordic area--Finland and Sweden, Norway, Denmark, and, farther away, Iceland--form the substance of this study. Geography and history have dictated entirely different contexts for those countries in their coexistence with the great neighbor.

The story of Finnish-Soviet relations during the past fifty years is repleat with animosity and conflict that was exorcised by a bloody war and followed by a stable but delicate relationship that has worked to mutual advantage, gradually wiping out the bitterness of defeat and human loss.

Sweden, on the other hand, has had a relationship with the U.S.S.R. that has been essentially free from serious conflict, although characterized at times by tension arising from a great power's "natural" tendency to assert its weight in the immediate vicinity and against a small, neutral state whose different outlook and social system might further complicate mutual comprehension.

Norway, fully independent since 1905, has had a common border with the Soviet Union since the end of the World War II. Relations have been dominated by the Soviet desire to deny any hostile power a foothold in the far North and in the Arctic. Large and outstanding territorial conflicts in the Barents Sea complicate the relationship, although cordiality has been normally retained by a certain restraint on both sides.

Denmark's principal interest from the Soviet perspective lies in its role as the guardian of the straits to and from the Baltic. As with Norway, Moscow's sensibility has been stung intermittently by suspected or actual Danish military cooperation with its Western allies--principally the U.S. and West Germany--but has been soothed by Danish regard for Soviet security interests.

Iceland is much farther away from Russia and forms part of a broader North Atlantic strategy. In this case, Soviet pressure must be applied or influence exercised from afar without the advantages of proximity.

What importance does Moscow attach to the Nordic countries? What future do Soviet policy makers desire for this region, and what are they prepared to accept? In which manner do they want to achieve their goals? What political tactics have proved to be useful? Are new factors emerging which change traditional Soviet policies toward this region?

The Nordic area is a big, sparsely populated piece of Europe directly adjacent to Russia's economic and political centers. The five Nordic states together are much larger than the U.K., France, and West Germany combined, but have only one-eighth of their population. Only eight countries in the world have larger GNPs than the Nordic group and this region is the second biggest trading partner of the U.S.S.R. in the capitalist world. The North Atlantic, geographically close to this area, has acquired great strategic significance and, recently, considerable economic interest through its oil and gas deposits.

Although Soviet leaders devote little time to Nordic problems, they pay more attention to them than other great powers. "Is not really the Soviet Union a Nordic country?" Kosygin asked at one meeting with Nordic leaders, mirroring an old Moscow desire to be treated differently and more favorably in this region than the other superpower. From its statements and actions, it can be deduced that Moscow would like to see the Nordic area as an entity linked in a symbiotic relationship to its great neighbor, the U.S.S.R. In Moscow's view, this area should thus be denied to competing protagonists and, ideally, kept separate from the rest of Europe. The individual Nordic countries should also be discouraged from forming any alliance of their own, political or military.

From the Soviet perspective, the pattern that has evolved in the region certainly could be improved. The status quo can, however, be accepted so long as the region is kept under constant supervision and pressure to counteract any negative developments. Vigilance is especially necessary against American or NATO machinations since the small Nordic states, by their weakness and Western links, are sensitive to persuasion from that quarter. While no automatic "balance" exists in the Nordic system, it is still true, say the Russians when it suits their purposes, that what one Nordic country does in its own security realm has a bearing on the situation of the others.

According to Moscow, pernicious outside influence in the region could be reduced if the Nordic countries all adopted neutrality guaranteed by the great powers. In the meantime, Finalnd serves as an illustration to the Scandinavians that a special relationship to the U.S.S.R. can very well be combined with neutrality. Stockholm in particular should emulate Helsinki. Both should help to persuade Denmark and Norway to go neutral, or to at least reduce dependence upon and services to the Western Alliance.

Moscow has maintained these attitudes for most of this fifty-year period, although Soviet policies have evolved over time reflecting leadership changes in Moscow as well as new strategic and political realities on the international scene. Various policy combinations have been tried, from the purely bilateral to more comprehensive regional efforts to influence the Scandinavians to move eastward in their political orientation.

Under Stalin, Finland was kept apart as a country with special links to the U.S.S.R. Soviet-Finnish relations indeed dominated Moscow's perspective of the Nordic region during the 1930s and 1940s. Finland's position was shaped by World War II and its immediate aftermath, and this in turn decided the political status of all Nordic countries.

In the postwar East-West conflict, Scandinavia, claiming nonalignment, was nonetheless initially treated by the U.S.S.R. as a member of the other camp, hostile and unreliable. Neutrality was not a desirable option. Up until the death of Stalin, the public diplomacy of the Soviet Union was characterized by harsh rhetoric on the struggle between capitalism and communism. The concept of two irreconcilable camps opposing each other shaped Soviet public diplomacy.

Actual Soviet behavior, however, only showed a determination
to have wartime advances recognized while cautiously trying to
limit the westward drift of neutral Nordic states. It was
important, too, to have a *cordon sanitaire* in the North. The
optimal result--a neutral, militarily divided Scandinavia--eluded
Moscow. Soviet distrust and political clumsiness contributed to
the decision of Norway and Denmark to join NATO, an event
that was grudgingly accepted by Moscow as a temporary
political fact, an "historical error."

The postwar political configuration in the Nordic area was
decided in essence by the early 1950s. The power pattern was
set. The spheres of interest had been defined and were to be
jealously guarded.

Khrushchev inaugurated detente in 1955. He approved of
neutrality both as a link between the camps and as a policy that
was likely to change in a positive direction as Soviet socialism
gained ground worldwide. The special *droit de regard* that the
U.S.S.R. proclaims as its right in respect to small and relatively
weak neighbors was, however, clearly exercised in the Nordic
area during the Khrushchev era. The flamboyant leader, riding
the crest of partly imagined Soviet successes and strengths,
sternly admonished the Scandinavian NATO members not to
provoke their powerful neighbor in their nuclear and military
base policies and counseled neutrality as a policy for the future.
Neutral Sweden was told fairly bluntly to cultivate its relations
with the East. The results of this policy of intermittent threats
and blandishments were uneven and most likely did not meet the
expectations of its optimistic author or of his cooler and more
conservative rivals. Expectations had to be reduced as
international tension, concentrated on Europe and Germany,
came to involve the Nordic region.

Khrushchev's successor in Moscow had a different
leadership style and other methods. The growth of Soviet
military power in the 1960s and 1970s did not result in increased
Soviet pressure for political change in Europe, but rather in a
more confident acceptance of the status quo combined with
suspicious attention to its adherence. Concurrently, military

positions were moved forward, in the far North and elsewhere. Perhaps political and military leaders in Moscow then came to expect more understanding of Soviet security interests on the part of the Nordic governments. Molotov probably expressed a general principle in Soviet foreign policy when he said to Sweden's ambassador to Moscow in 1943: "The foreign policy of the U.S.S.R. must be shaped according to its increased military strength."

Detente, however, began to evolve and the focus of international conflicts moved from Europe to the Third World. All this helped to establish relative calm in the Nordic region until the late 1970s.

New tension between the superpowers, uncertainty about military developments in Europe, and the increased strategic significance of the North Atlantic and the European far north have since combined to complicate the Soviet relationship with the Scandinavians. Finland on the other hand has managed to stay out of the disputes and has maintained for about a quarter of a century a very cordial and fairly relaxed relationship with her great neighbor.

For the future, there is a common strategic denominator to Moscow's Scandinavian troubles. While the U.S.S.R. conducts a special bilateral policy for each of these countries and only occasionally sees reason to propound its vision for the Nordic region as a whole, military planning might have to encompass them all. New factors will influence peace and security in the North. Nuclear parity on all levels might increase the risks of conventional war in Europe and intensify the military interest in the Nordic area. Strategic developments, in which submarines carrying nuclear missiles play a major role, concentrate attention on the principal Soviet naval base on the Kola Peninsula and thus on the Scandinavian north. East-West tension makes these developments dangerous.

Chapter 1

WAR DIPLOMACY

FINLAND, SWEDEN, AND RUSSIA: A RHAPSODIC HISTORY

Policies toward Finland and Sweden, the principal partners in the Nordic region, demonstrate the powerful strain of continuity in Russian attitudes. Sketching a few highlights in the history of this relationship is therefore warranted.

Historically, changes in the eastern borders of Finland, until 1809 part of the Swedish realm, have reflected shifts in the balance of power between Sweden and Russia. In periods of Russian weakness, the border was pushed east and south. At the peak of its power, Sweden sought and achieved hegemony in the Baltic, driving Russia from its shores (the peace of Stolbova in 1617). The roles in Northern Europe changed as Russia increased its military strength under Peter I. Access to the sea and to shipping routes were the basis for Russia's ambitions to dominate the Baltic and the Black Sea. In subsequent peace treaties after Swedish defeats in "The Great Northern War," the border moved steadily westward. Peter wanted security for his new capital of St. Petersburg, built as a demonstration of his determination to control this area, an outlet to the West.

Alexander I, twice defeated by Napoleon, agreed at Tilsit in 1807 to take part in the blockade against Britain, obtaining in return a free hand in Finland. Control of the northern shore of the Gulf of Finland would have been sufficient to secure Russian defense needs and, indeed, Alexander seems to have had no plans to conquer all of Finland or to annex it. But Russian troops were initially allowed to advance almost unopposed, and the tsar came to expand his objective and seek to join all of Finland to the Russian empire. The spirited resistance to this campaign later put up by the Finns themselves and Alexander's fear that Napoleon would once again turn against Russia ultimately forced the tsar to recognize Finnish nationhood and an autonomous status for Finland within the Russian realm.

Finland's fortunes within the empire fluctuated in the 19th century depending on the autocrat in power in St. Petersburg. Russian nationalism, whose major objective was the unification of the Slavs, was dormant for most of this time. As for Finland, Russian rulers were primarily concerned with defense and power politics in Europe. As long as the Finns remained loyal and appreciated the advantages of union with Russia (such as splendid career possibilities in the Russian bureaucracy, army, and navy), they were essentially left to govern themselves. The shockwaves from the revolutions of 1830 and 1848, however, turned St. Petersburg's attention to nascent nationalist and revolutionary movements and led to suppression and reaction which also hit Finland. Further trouble came during the Crimean War when British and French naval forces revealed the decline of Russia's power by shelling with impunity the Finnish coastline. Finnish loyalty to the tsar during his dilemma was this time rewarded with further liberalization.

The Swedes, at this time, came into direct conflict with Russia. The first of the Bernadottes, Karl XIV Johan (1810/1818-44), a Frenchman with a keen sense of political realities, had realized that Sweden's role as a great power was long since gone. Shifting his allegiances, he had formed an alliance with Russia and Great Britain and helped to defeat Napoleon. The loss of Finland and the Aland Islands was somewhat offset by the victory over Denmark in 1814 by which Sweden gained control of Norway. Karl XIV Johan had adopted "a strong and independent neutrality" as the guiding principle for Swedish foreign policy in wartime. His successors, less astute in matters of state, abandoned an important part of this policy, the careful cultivation of relations with Russia. Instead, airy schemes were once again brought to life to reestablish Sweden's old position of power in Northern Europe. These schemes undercut the policy, dear to Karl Johan, not to complicate Finland's effort to uphold its autonomy, since suspicions in St. Petersburg of Swedish intentions could lead the Russians to take firmer control over Finland.

The new Swedish king, Oscar I, did not proceed nearly as prudently as Karl Johan. During the Crimean War, he declared Swedish readiness to enter on the side of the Western powers if Swedish war goals were recognized. He encouraged anti-Russian propaganda in Sweden and negotiated an agreement with England and France whereby they guaranteed the security of Sweden and Norway against Russia, provided no land was willingly given up or sold to Russia (the British feared that the Russians wanted to acquire ports in northern Norway). As a next step, a formal alliance was planned with Swedish participation in a large offensive in the Baltic.

Before these far-reaching plans were realized, the Crimean War came to an end. Stockholm had by then already opened up Swedish ports on the Baltic to British-French flottillas operating against Russian shipping and against harbors and fortified positions in Finland as part of a scheme to encourage the presence of Western warships in the Baltic to redress the balance of power. While permitting the use of neutral ports by battleships did not legally break neutrality rules, it obviously created irritation and distrust against Sweden in St. Petersburg.

The end of the 19th century saw the growth of Russian chauvinism coupled with an increasing fear of Germany. Sympathy toward Sweden by some groups in Finland, plus Russian fears that Sweden would ally itself with Germany, fortified the trend toward more repressive Russian policies. Demands were made within Russia for russification and an end to Finland's special status. At the turn of the century, this became official policy, but defeats in the war against Japan and uprisings in Russia forced the tsar to relax his grip and even grant new steps toward democracy.

Soon, however, St. Petersburg began again to increase its oppression and systematically deprive Finland of her constitutional rights. A clear separation from Russia appeared to be the only means of preserving Finnish national existence. Russian defeat at German hands in World War I offered the possibility for Finnish independence. When the revolution brought the Bolsheviks to power, they recognized and accepted Finland's declaration of independence. While this recognition was true to their doctrines of self-determination for the nationalities in the Russian empire, the Bolsheviks in fact hoped for the victory of the revolutionary forces in Finland. Lenin signed the recognition of Finnish independence, but Stalin declared after recognition that the Council of Peoples' Commissars had been forced against its will to grant Finland independence because the proletariat "had failed to take power due to vacillation and inexplicable timidity." The Soviet government recognized a Finnish revolutionary leadership created by Finnish socialists, and Russian troops provided them with arms and some military support in an attempted revolt against the newly elected government. However, Russian support was insufficient to tip the balance of strength in the bloody civil war that followed, which likewise was not greatly influenced by the late arrival of German military support for the bourgeois government.

The Conservative government which thus came to power in Helsinki established close ties with Germany, both as a guarantee against possible Russian action and as a potential aid in the conquest of East Karelia, an area formed by Lake Ladoga, Lake Onega, and the White Sea. The German defeat in World War I ended these hopes and the plans for German-Finnish cooperation. A new government in Finland abandoned its German connection, sought Western aid, and even toyed for a while with the idea, later abandoned, of joining in the anti-Bolshevik intervention attacking Petrograd.

The hard-pressed Soviet government, which had had to suffer some fairly extravagant demands from former Russian satellites, offered repeatedly to make peace with the western borderlands. Finland maintained that its negotiations with the Soviets should be held at the same time as those with the Baltic states. Treaties were concluded by the Soviets in 1920 with all the Baltic countries, and on generous terms at that, and the Finns started peace talks in mid-1920.

The Bolsheviks, who had survived the most dangerous threats to their continued rule, firmly rejected the most excessive Finnish demands and put forth some of their own. The Finns sought expansion, asking for all of East Karelia, including the Kola Peninsula. The Russians refused and demanded economic concessions but, after considerable bargaining, conceded Petsamo, up in the very north, giving the Finns access to the Arctic Ocean and enhancing the "Nordic" quality of Finland over the purely "Baltic" one. The Finns had to give up any claims on East Karelia and be content with the border of autonomous Finland that had been established in 1812. The peace of Tartu (Dorpat) was vehemently attacked by the right-wing opposition in Finland, adding a revanchist aspect to the bilateral relations. Russia, on its hand, was pushed back, in Finland and in the Baltic area as a whole, to positions it had occupied in the 17th century. Two hundred years of costly expansion were nullified.

Relations were further complicated in the 1920s and early 1930s by the meanderings of Finnish foreign policy as conducted by Conservative, German-oriented presidents who were generally hostile to the Soviet Union. They encouraged close cooperation with Estonia, Lithuania, Latvia, and Poland, the border states immediately to the south of the U.S.S.R. These nations had broken away from Russia in the aftermath of World War I but their strategic location and historical background were such that they were obvious objects of great-power (i.e., German and Soviet) *convoitise*. An alliance with these states could not guarantee Finland any mutual aid but would only involve her in awkward entanglements. On Polish insistence, however, the Finnish government adhered to the alliance, but it was disavowed by the Finnish parliament, which stressed the Scandinavian option and opposed action that could be seen as directed against Finland's ever-mightier neighbor. The past, however, was laden with suspicion and mistrust.

The Scandinavian Countries and Russia until
World War II

Sweden managed to steer a neutral and independent course during the First World War. At the outset of hostilities, Norway and Denmark joined with Sweden to proclaim neutrality and Scandinavian unity. The great powers in the war, including Russia, promised to respect Swedish integrity and independence, provided that Sweden remained neutral. Germany insisted on and received promises from Stockholm of "a benevolent neutrality." Accordingly, Sweden prohibited the transport of arms through its territory to Russia and joined Denmark in mining the exits from and entrances to the Baltic. The Russian military, however, were skeptical of Swedish neutrality because of the central role that Finland played in Swedish policies toward Russia. Russian war plans reflected the military's suspicions that Sweden would participate in the war on the side of Germany by joint naval operations in the Baltic or even by combined troop landings in Finland that could threaten St. Petersburg. In Sweden, "the Russian menace" was much talked about and the tsar was credited with sinister plans to grab ice-free ports on the Atlantic. No such plans materialized and relations remained fairly cordial all through the war.

For most of the period between the two world wars, Sweden had only superficial contact with the Soviet Union. The Russian revolution and its aftermath had changed the political map in the Baltic area. In the place of the tsarist empire, long feared and respected as the powerful neighbor to the east, came the Soviet Union, initially a chaotic and weak state whose influence reached into the Baltic only in the innermost part of the Finnish Gulf. Sweden was thus shielded from the U.S.S.R. not only by Finland but also by the three Baltic republics.

During the 1930s, as the Soviet Union grew in power and ambitions, the question of Finland returned as the key to Soviet-Swedish relations. While Finland's political orientation, which from the mid-1930s became increasingly Nordic, was accepted by Moscow, it did not countenance any concrete Finnish military cooperation with Sweden. This position was based on the idea that Germany's growing strength and aggressiveness might make it necessary for the Soviet Union to safeguard its northwestern flank by military means, and that this might be more easily accomplished if Finland were isolated from the other Nordic countries. In Sweden, opinions were divided as to how active a policy should be pursued, but prudence prevailed and dictated a skeptical attitude toward a Finnish-Swedish defense alliance. On the key question of the Aland Islands in the Baltic, where the Finns wanted a joint defense arrangement, the Swedes were willing to accept obligations only if all interested great powers were agreed, including the U.S.S.R. Stockholm backed away as Moscow became increasingly negative to such an arrangement and began to engage Finland in Soviet-Finnish bilateral security discussions.

General international reasons had earlier motivated Moscow to launch a virulent attack on the Nordic countries' efforts in the late 1930s to declare neutrality as a common policy. This was a "cowardly political line which would only help the aggressor, Germany." The Soviet line at this time was to strengthen the collective security system of the League of Nations and to build an anti-fascist alliance. Thus, neutrality had to be attacked.

Norway's relations with Russia had traditionally been friendly, without the entrenched suspicion of that country which prevailed in Sweden. The Russians had long been seen as a counterweight against the Swedes; they favored the dissolution of the union between the two countries and were the first great power to recognize Norway's independence in 1905. After the 1917 revolution, the Norwegian Labor party, which was going through a period of radicalism, joined the Moscow-led Third International, and was the only major social democratic party in

Western Europe to do so. The party remained in the International until 1923. After bitter feuding with the Communist party, the Labor party shifted course and gradually established itself as Norway's dominant party left of the center. By 1930 the Communists had been reduced to insignificance in Norwegian politics and were to remain so until the present day, as indeed has been the case all along in the other Scandinavian countries. Events in the Soviet Union in the 1930s and the Finnish-Russian war of 1939-40 further alienated the Labor party leadership from the Soviet Union and the local Communists.

As to the security relationship between Norway and the U.S.S.R., the strategically exposed position of the province of Finnmark in northeastern Norway--with a population of less than 60,000 and an area 50 percent larger than the Netherlands--had been a source of concern for Scandinavian as well as British governments. They feared that Russia, which would be largely unopposed in this region, might try to extend its short ice-free northern coastline to gain harbors which would effectively make it an Atlantic power. (Udgaard, p. 20.)

Denmark had had only minimal relations with the Soviet Union during the 1920s and 1930s. As was later revealed by the positive Soviet reaction to the German occupation of Denmark and Norway in 1940 and in Soviet dealings with the British allies, these two Scandinavian countries were placed outside the immediate Soviet sphere of interest and were important mainly as guardians of essential water lanes.

DIPLOMATIC PREPARATIONS FOR THE WAR

In Stalin's complicated schemes to avoid and/or prepare for war at the end of the 1930s, the Nordic area and the Baltic came to play a considerable role. For Russia, whose situation up until the autumn of 1939 still looked dim and menaced, it was important to gain defensive buffer territory in the northwest around its second city, Leningrad.

Speaking in 1936, Zhdanov, the Leningrad party boss and later Stalin's "crown prince," sounded one of the first warnings of troubles to come:

> The Leningrad region marks the Soviet frontier with Finland, Estonia, and Latvia, countries with whose people the U.S.S.R. has normal, peaceful relations. . . . And if in some of these little countries, for example Finland, feelings of hostility to the U.S.S.R. are being kindled by larger and more adventurist countries and preparations are being made to make their territory available for aggressive action by fascist powers, in the long run it is these little countries alone which will be the losers. It does not pay for little countries to get entangled in big adventures. (Degras, p. 226.)

Tass, however, hastened to issue a revised version of this statement in which fascism, and not the Baltic states, was blamed. Official Soviet foreign policy at the time tried to please and reassure, not threaten or provoke, the small neighbors. Zhdanov's remarks indicated a more aggressive option based upon the belief that Finland surely would be the ally of Germany in attacks from the north against Leningrad.

The Finnish president at the time, Svinhufvud, had represented the pro-German orientation in Finland. Exiled to Siberia by the tsar for his fight against Russian oppression, he returned to Finland in the wake of the Bolshevik revolution to lead the movement for independence. In 1918 he had tried to install a German prince as the monarch of Finland, and in 1930 he had expelled the Finnish Communists from parliament and forced them to go underground. He took a dim view of Finnish-Soviet relations and was thus an exponent of one line of thinking--hard-headed but, as it turned out, not very circumspect about German interests and capabilities, perhaps excessively pessimistic about Soviet intentions. "Russia's enemy must always be the friend of Finland," he told a German visitor in 1937, "for an independent Finland is a permanent threat to Leningrad and this threat can be removed only through the annexation of Finland. Russian assurances and treaties cannot change this fact. . . . In time of need only Germany can help Finland."

No wonder that the Russians hailed the defeat in the 1937 presidential elections of this "important card in Berlin's diplomatic-military game." Svinhufvud's successors initially tried to improve relations with Moscow, with such success that the Russians started to treat Finnish emissaries almost as potential allies. In the spring of 1938 the Soviet Union made an overture. Yartsev, an embassy official of low rank, put forth ideas which were later followed up by Foreign Minister Litvinov. Yartsev's proposals were reported by Tanner, a leader of the Social Democrats who was directly involved in these discussions:

> The Russian government wished to respect Finland's independence and territorial integrity, but Moscow was wholly convinced that Germany entertained such extensive plans of aggression against Russia that the objective of the extreme left wing of the German armies would be to effect a landing in Finland and thence to plunge their attack into Russia. At that time, there would arise the question of what attitude Finland should assume toward these German intentions. If Germany were allowed to carry out these operations in Finland unopposed, Russia would not passively await the German arrival at Rajajoki but would throw its armed forces as far into Finland as possible, whereupon the battles between German and Russian forces would take place on Finnish territory. If, instead, Finland were to oppose the German landings, Russia would offer Finland all possible economic and military assistance, binding itself to withdraw its forces from Finland after the war.

The Russians required at least a written understanding under which Finland declared its readiness to ward off possible attacks and, to that end, accept Russian military aid. This would not necessarily mean dispatch of military forces or territorial concessions. As a "return favor," Moscow wanted Finnish consent to set up on Suursaari (Hogland) Island in the Finnish Gulf close to Leningrad a fortified air and naval base. Finland rejected the proposals and assured the Russians that it was determined to defend its neutrality under all circumstances.

At the same time, the U.S.S.R. was engaged in other negotiations about the Baltic area. Moscow proposed in April 1939 that Great Britain, France, and the Soviet Union undertake to render military aid to any East European country between the Baltic and the Black Sea bordering the Soviet Union. The Soviet draft applied principally to Latvia and Estonia but also to Finland, which was counted, against prevailing practices, among the Baltic states. Such Soviet guarantees, which were later said to apply also in the case of "indirect aggression," would authorize almost unlimited interference in the internal affairs of those three countries.

The background to this proposal can be seen as early as 1935 in Stalin's speech which warned of "the new German policy" reminiscent of the policy of the former German Kaiser, "who marched against Leningrad and converted the Baltic countries into a *place d'armes* for this march." As Molotov said to the French ambassador, the Soviet Union, treaty or no treaty, would be compelled to "come to the assistance" of the three Baltic states even without their request "if one or more of them want to sell itself to Germany" (Taralis, p. 105). The Baltic states protested vigorously in Western capitals, and as a result no agreement was reached.

How did the Finns reason in the face of this mounting political and military threat? Those with the most experience with Russia, Mannerheim, Paasikivi, Enckell--old men who had known from the inside the tsarist great power before the First World War--were of the view that Finland should have shown more flexibility in the negotiations. Field Marshal Mannerheim had above all a keen sense of Russian military thinking from his own service as a general in the tsarist army. "The ladies of St.

Petersburg could not sleep peacefully as long as the Finnish
frontier ran so close to our capital," wrote Peter the Great, and
Mannerheim could appreciate this explanation of military conquests. Perhaps, like Alexander I, the Russians want the Finnish
coastline to the south, he said to Paasikivi. Paradoxically,
Mannerheim, who in Moscow was seen as an implacable enemy
of communism and the Soviet state, urged the government not to
let the Soviets leave empty-handed. The islands that Moscow
asked for had no military value for Finland. To Russia, on the
other hand, they were important. Giving them up was a small
price to pay for Russia's good will in other matters, above all
the Aland question. Only Soviet acquiescence would make
possible a Swedish-Finnish defense pact which would permit
neutrality in the war to come between the great powers.
Anticipating Moscow's later demands, Mannerheim even
suggested that the frontier on the Karelian Isthmus be moved
further north from Leningrad.

Mannerheim and Paasikivi shared the same basic pessimistic
attitude. The political system in Europe had collapsed and in
this situation major upheavals must be feared, in which the
great powers would act, as they always do, with brutality,
lawlessness, and according to their own narrowly conceived
interests--according to Bismarck, "the only sound basis for great
power behavior."

This pessimism seemed to mark the basic distinction
between the different actors on the Finnish scene. The
dominant thinking in Helsinki up until the war broke out was
that no statesman would be so foolish as to start a new major
war. This dominant group (Tanner *et al.)* also had a more
benign view of the Soviet propensity for aggression ("The
Russians do not plan conquests, they are only concerned about
their own security"). They therefore quite logically saw less
need to satisfy Moscow's territorial demands, believing that
promises and declarations of neutrality were enough and
overlooking the imminent threat.

The importance of international law, of the League of
Nations, and of treaties and agreements between states was

referred to by this group. In more pragmatic moments, Russian strength was considered but underestimated. Most important and difficult perhaps was the question, recurring all through later years: Would not concessions now lead to fresh demands later?

This group seems to have given no deep thought to a theme that much preoccupied Paasikivi, i.e., the innate imperialist and expansionist nature of great powers: "The need for expansion seems to be a dark force of nature in the life of great powers. All great powers are imperialistic. Such has been the case with the Russian realm all through the centuries." Paasikivi, as related in his memoirs, also discussed the Nordic area in the strategic concept of Moscow:

> Conquest of Finland must be secondary to Russia. The limited goal of defense of Russia's northwestern borders could be achieved in another manner. However, an ambition to reach the Atlantic would be characteristic of (Russian) imperialism. . . . A realization of Russia's aspirations toward the Atlantic would lead to a tremendous expansion and fortifying of the military position of the great power. A Russia, controlling northern Scandinavia and the outlying ocean areas, the Atlantic and the Arctic Ocean, would play a totally different role in world politics than before. The possession of Finland alone would not entail such benefits. In case Russia has such imperialist ambitions, the fate of Finland and Sweden are closely linked.

Paasikivi, however, moderated his pessimistic speculations about the innate imperialism of great powers by pointing out that such farflung ambitions had not at any time been explicit Russian policy. All that was known about Soviet intentions could in reality be described as a fairly moderate defense posture in the face of foreseeable German aggression.

The idea of a military alliance between the U.S.S.R. and Finland was clearly apparent in Yartsev's discussions with the Finns. Helsinki, however, pointed out that Finland wanted neutrality with a Scandinavian orientation. The implication of

the Soviet answer was that Finland could well play at being
Scandinavian and neutral in times of peace as long as she
promised to be Baltic and a Soviet ally in times of war
(Jacobson, p. 49). The Finns obviously could not accept this
reasoning, as neutrality had the precise aim of keeping the
country out of war.

The Soviet pressure had little impact at this time because it
seemed, after Munich, that the U.S.S.R. had been isolated, that
Germany was the dominant power on the European continent,
and that reconciliation was possible between the Western powers
and Germany. Of course, those who claim that Helsinki chose
the wrong policy argue that this was precisely the moment to
strike a deal with the Russians.

The nonaggression pact of 23 August 1939 between
Germany and the Soviet Union, amended in the Molotov-
Ribbentrop accord of 29 September in Moscow, established a
whole new set of rules for the northwestern neighbors of the
U.S.S.R. The agreements in the secret protocols gave to Russia
the eastern territories of Poland and a free hand in Estonia,
Latvia, Lithuania, and Finland, as being in its "sphere of
influence." It was now no longer necessary for Moscow to retain
the Western option or to take into account negative British or
French reaction to any move against the small neighboring
states.

The alliance between the two dictators was based, however,
on a very temporary convenience. Stalin had no doubts about
Hitler's long-range plans and clearly said and acted so in the
immediate aftermath. The problem was how long Berlin would
be kept busy by its Western enemies and how best to prepare for
a change in political fortunes. The territorial rearrangements
that Moscow now embarked upon flowed both from the need to
bolster its defensive posture in preparation for a coming German
onslaught and from a desire for imperial expansion made
possible at low cost and low risk by the Nazi-Soviet pact. Each
particular case had a different mixture of motives. Apart from
considerations of a permanent nature, such as historical ties,
economic and strategic significance, etc., Moscow had to watch

carefully that its actions would not unduly antagonize Hitler nor involve the U.S.S.R. in a war against the Western Allies. At the same time, Stalin had to work fast to avert any surprises that the Germans might have in store.

Western Byelo-Russia and Western Ukraine were speedily annexed to the corresponding Soviet republics, thus becoming integral parts of the U.S.S.R. As the Polish events started to unfold, Moscow demanded that the Baltic states send their foreign ministers to Moscow for negotiations. The negotiations were brief. Soon, each of these countries concluded treaties of friendship and reciprocal aid with the U.S.S.R., granting at the same time air and naval bases to the Soviet Union and a considerable presence of Soviet troops. If these countries had had any plans to resist, those were presumably dispelled by the massive troop concentration along the borders of Estonia and Latvia and repeated violations of their airspace and waters. Although the Baltic negotiators did achieve some reduction in the Russian demands, in essence they were met with ultimata combined with threats to use military force.

All sorts of reasons were given by the Soviet side to justify the peremptory demands. A *Tass* report claimed, for example, that "periscopes of unknown submarines have been seen," which led to the conclusion that "not far from the Estonian shore some unknown submarines have a secret base which give the question of safeguarding the security of Soviet waters against diversionist acts on the part of foreign submarines in hiding great importance" (*Pravda*, 27 September 1939). In the negotiations, Molotov took a stern, uncompromising approach while Stalin softened this harsh impression by some minor concessions and by frank explanations of the realities involved. It was assumed that these small states, even if they had the will, did not have the capacity to maintain and protect their neutrality. In essence, the Russian position was, "we cannot permit small states to be used against the U.S.S.R. Neutral Baltic states--that is too insecure." The Soviet Union, however, acquired more than "security" by its pacts with the Baltic states. From the naval bases the Soviets now controlled, units of the Soviet fleet could henceforth fight battles at very short notice and take on offensive tasks in the major part of the Baltic.

A few weeks after these negotiations were concluded, Helsinki received a similarly worded invitation. In Moscow, the Finns were met with well-known arguments. A written memorandum gave "the principal concerns of the Soviet Union in its negotiations with Finland" (Tanner, p. 29):

> a) guarantees for the safety of Leningrad,

> b) assurance that Finland will, on a basis of friendly relationship, come to maintain a close association with the Soviet Union. Both parts are indispensable in order to safeguard the Soviet shore of the Gulf of Finland.

> In order to carry out this undertaking it is necessary:

> 1. That the Soviet Union be enabled to close the mouth of the Gulf of Finland through artillery fire from both shores, so that hostile naval and merchant vessels may be barred from the waters of the Gulf of Finland;

> 2. That the Soviet Union be enabled to prevent the access of an enemy to those islands of the Gulf of Finland which lie along the channels west and northwest of Leningrad;

> 3. That the Finnish boundary on the Karelian Isthmus, which is now at thirty-two kilometers from Leningrad (that is to say, within reach of shells from long-range cannon), be moved somewhat farther north and northwest.

> Separately there arises the question of the Rybachi Peninsula at Petsamo, where the boundary is ineptly and artificially drawn and where it should be corrected in accordance with the attached map.

Stalin's thinking on this matter seemed clear as he spoke to Paasikivi, the Finnish negotiator, who had also led his country's delegation to the 1920 peace talks. The great war now in progress required measures to obtain complete security, said the

Soviet leader. If the views of the military command were to be accepted, the Soviets would have to call for the boundary existing at the time of Peter the Great. (This boundary was later established by the peace treaty after the war.) The conversation went on:

> "It is not the fault of either of us that geographical circumstances are as they are. We must be able to bar entrance to the Gulf of Finland. If the channel to Leningrad did not run along your coast, we would not have had the slightest occasion to bring the matter up. We must bear in mind also the worst possible eventualities. Tsarist Russia had the Porkkala and Naissaari fortresses with their twelve-inch guns, and the Tallinn naval base as well. At that time it was impossible for an enemy to come through the breach. We do not ask either for Porkkala or for Naissaari, as they are too near the capitals of Finland and Estonia. On the other hand, an effective seal can be created between Hanko and Paldiski.

> "It is a law of naval strategy that passage into the Gulf of Finland can be blocked by the cross fire of batteries of both shores as far out as the mouth of the Gulf. Your memorandum supposes that an enemy cannot penetrate into the Gulf. But once a hostile fleet is in the Gulf, the Gulf can no longer be defended.

> "You ask what power might attack us, England or Germany. We are on good terms with Germany now, but everything in this world may change. Yudenich attacked through the Gulf of Finland and later the British did the same. This can happen again. If you are afraid to give us bases on the mainland, we can dig a canal across Hanko Neck, and then our base won't be on Finnish mainland territory. As things stand now, both England and Germany can send large naval units into the Gulf of Finland. I doubt whether you would be able to avoid an incident in that case. England is pressuring Sweden for bases right now. Germany is doing likewise. When the war between those two is over, the victor's fleet will come into the Gulf.

"You ask, why do we want Koivisto? I'll tell
you why. I asked Ribbentrop why Germany
went to war with Poland. He replied, 'We had to
move the Polish border farther from Berlin.'
Before the war the distance from Poznan to
Berlin was about two hundred kilometers. Now
the border has been moved three hundred
kilometers farther east. We ask that the distance
from Leningrad to the line should be seventy
kilometers. That is our minimum demand, and
you must not think we are prepared to reduce it
bit by bit. We can't move Leningrad, so the line
has to move. Regarding Koivisto, you must bear
in mind that if sixteen-inch guns were placed
there they could entirely prevent movements of
our fleet in the inmost extremity of the Gulf.
We ask for 2,700 square kilometers and offer
more than 5,500 in exchange. Does any other
great power do that? No. We are the only ones
that simple."

The Finns proved adamant in their opposition to Soviet
demands. Stalin, who participated practically all through the
negotiations, which lasted one month from early October,
repeatedly tried new formulas and drew new boundary lines
freehand on the general staff map on the table in front of the
delegations, displaying a detailed knowledge of the geography of
the area. The conversations were often "light and friendly," and
the Russians seemed genuinely astonished at Finnish stubbornness and vexed when the Finns claimed that warfare would not
occur in the vicinity of the Gulf of Finland nor perhaps on the
shores of the Arctic Ocean. Mikoyan told Tanner at a reception
that

when the Cabinet (sic) had discussed the terms to
be offered Finland it was generally thought that
easy conditions should be offered. They all had
great respect for Finland. There was a saying
'Finskij narod, tvordij narod' ('The Finns are a
tough people') which accordingly had to be
treated with circumspection. If there were just
Russians in our government things would be quite
different. But Stalin is a Georgian, I am an

Armenian, and many of the rest are minority nationals. We understand the position of a small country very well.

"Let's drop all sentimental matters," Molotov said much later to Paasikivi when the Finnish negotiator tried to invoke Lenin and Stalin as early supporters of Finnish independence. That probably better reflected Politburo discussions. Stalin himself showed clear irritation as he received a Finnish *njet* to his final proposal in the talks. Pointing at a new and smaller island (Russaro) and asking, "Could you perhaps let go of this islet?" the dictator of the vast Soviet empire had to conclude despondently after the Finnish refusal, "Then it does not look as anything will come out of it. Nothing will come out of it." The Finnish negotiators took their leave in a friendly atmosphere. "Good luck," said Stalin.

The Winter War and Its Aftermath

Illusions were built on these amical moments, but they were quickly shattered. A campaign against Finland was started in the press; border incidents occurred; Soviet demands were made for a one-sided Finnish troop withdrawal to twenty-five kilometers from the border; a Soviet statement declared that as a result of Finnish provocations, the U.S.S.R. regarded itself as freed from the nonaggression pact between the two countries; Soviet diplomatic staff was recalled--all this preceded the Soviet attack on Finland, without a declaration of war, a few weeks later on 30 November. Two days later, the U.S.S.R. and the "People's Government of Finland," a Soviet puppet regime set up under O. V. Kuusinen, concluded a treaty of mutual assistance that gave the Soviet Union the territories it had asked for and, ironically, incorporated into Finland the main part of Soviet Karelia. If Kuusinen came to rule Finland, the Soviet leaders must have reasoned, such geographic delimitation would be of no importance.

Contrary to all expectations, the Finns managed to stop the Russian offensive, inflict heavy casualties, and stabilize the front until the beginning of February 1940. The French and the British were for various reasons interested in sending some troop contingents through Sweden to Finland. Neither presumably really wanted war with Russia added to their troubles. London and Paris had shown in July/August 1939 that, if necessary, they would agree to place Finland within the Russian orbit. The heroic Finnish resistance in the Winter War, however, generated broad public support in France and Britain, including demands for government action to aid that little embattled country. At the same time, the Western powers had an interest in moving troop aid to Finland, channeled through Sweden, as a stratagem to take possession of the Swedish iron-ore mines, whose deliveries were important for the German war machine. Grandiose plans for such operations were made and widely talked about.

The Russians may have seen through the West's ulterior motives and lack of realism (the Swedes were adamantly opposed to any foreign troops on their territory, and the British and the French could only send small contingents of little military value, so as not to weaken the Central front). Moscow sensed, however, that the Finns counted on the potential aid. Desire to avoid becoming embroiled in a wider conflict that included Britain and France must have contributed to the Soviet decision to make up with Finland on much less than maximal terms. The doctrine of "revolution by bayonet" had been practiced in the early years of Soviet rule in Georgia, Outer Mongolia, and other areas. Now, however, Stalin acted in the interests of the Soviet Union as a great international power, and not in the service of an abstract notion of revolution accomplished by Soviet arms. Without much ado, the Kuusinen "government" slipped into limbo, which was easy enough since Moscow had never tried to get even German recognition of it. The Finns sued for peace and accepted the territorial concessions demanded.

The Winter War had ended. The Russians, however, had learned that the Finns were tougher than their small Baltic neighbors, a lesson that came at a time when the Soviets were not free to carry on the war for too long. The Soviet Union had gained some military positions, which turned out to be of no value whatsoever in the war to come, but it paid a heavy price by turning its neighbor into a revanchist enemy and, more importantly, by giving the world, particularly the Germans, a false image of a militarily impotent giant.

SOVIET ATTITUDES TOWARD SWEDEN, 1939-1941

Sweden was not an important factor in early Soviet considerations of its relations with Finland, and was given scant atten-
tion by Moscow. Before the Soviet-German pact, Sweden and the other Scandinavian countries had been admonished by the Soviet Union to take a firmer negative attitude toward Germany, but Soviet officials also paid their respects to the neutrality policy of these countries. When the Finnish-Soviet negotiations were underway in October 1939, Molotov referred publicly to "nonsensical talk about . . . alleged claims of the Soviet Union against Sweden and Norway" and "lies that the Soviet Union demands the Aland Islands."

Indeed, no such claims were made. As to the Aland Islands, Finnish territory in the Baltic between Finland and Sweden, Moscow alternately objected to all Finnish-Swedish cooperative projects for a defense buildup on the islands; claimed a right to military presence in this area (Yartsev, 1938), or at least a right equal to Sweden's on this score; agreed to Finnish--but only Finnish--fortifications on the islands (1939); and demanded in 1940 that these fortifications be dismantled and that a large Soviet consulate be permitted there. Possession of a military base on the Aland Islands would constitute a direct threat to the Swedish capital, but no such Soviet demands were ever made. Thus, Soviet behavior through this period hardly constituted proof of aggressive intentions in this area. Indeed, their main concern at the time was to avoid having Sweden drawn into the war on Finland's side via Aland.

The main strand of Soviet thinking was all along to disassociate Sweden from Finland and to regard all Swedish interest in Soviet-Finnish relations as unwarranted interference. Molotov refused to accept a Swedish note in early November 1939 which stressed the importance for Sweden of Finland's continued independence and neutrality. This is, said the foreign commissar to the Swedish ambassador, an inimical act against the U.S.S.R., an effort to lead Finland astray, a plan to form a bloc hostile to the Soviet Union. That game could be dangerous for Sweden. The next day, in a *Pravda* article ascribed by Moscow observers to Stalin himself, Swedish politicians were portrayed as henchmen for Western interests trying to sabotage Soviet security in the Finnish Gulf. Molotov, in fact, had only echoed his predecessor, Litvinov, who, six months earlier, more politely but nonetheless firmly rejected Swedish comments on the then topical Finnish-Soviet talks. These were matters which concerned only Finland and the U.S.S.R., Litvinov had said, and Sweden should learn not to stick its little nose into a Soviet sphere of interest. Moscow probably believed at the time that Stockholm strengthened the Finnish will to resist the Soviet demands.

Stockholm refrained from declaring neutrality in the Winter War and massive Swedish assistance was given to Finland's military efforts. Eight thousand Swedish volunteers served in the Finnish armed forces. These were obviously factors that weighed negatively in Swedish-Soviet relations. In later phases, during the two wars, Sweden's good offices were mostly welcome, particularly as Sweden was known to counsel acceptance of the distasteful but unavoidable reality of Russian power.

Sweden and Russia had some interests that ran parallel. In early 1940, the Swedes were afraid lest the British-French "aid expedition to Finland" draw Sweden into the war, as was in fact its main purpose. With the outsider's more dispassionate and sometimes more realistic analysis of the relation of forces, the

Swedes therefore urged the Finns to consider concessions in the face of adversity and make up with Moscow, even if that meant accepting harsh conditions. Had the Russians persisted in dealing only with its own puppet government, the situation would obviously have been different and the Swedes would have had to make a much more dramatic decision. In early 1940, Moscow had, however, already dropped Kuusinen. The issue was then no longer Finland's existence, an existential matter for Sweden and the Swedes, but Finland's borders, or, more precisely, one-tenth of its territory. For this stake, Sweden, which had received troop requests from Finland, was unwilling to intervene.

Stockholm was likewise determined to prevent the Finnish border issue from becoming a basis for Western intervention in the area, provoking a German counterattack and a major war on Swedish soil. "Objectively," both these positions were obviously also in the Russian interest. The Swedish diplomatic game was complex. While giving the Finns all possible material aid and permitting volunteers, Sweden had to tell the Finns that they should rely neither on Swedish intervention nor on British-French troops, but make up with Stalin. Moscow should be left uncertain about Swedish intentions on either matter so as to make it more willing to compromise. The Germans were to be assured that no danger was in store for their iron-ore deliveries, and the British and the French must be persuaded that their project to intervene in the North would be counterproductive, impermissible, and impossible. Obviously, all this could not fully succeed. The Finns complained bitterly, the Germans intervened themselves in Norway and Denmark--partly to offset the risk of a British landing in the North--and the British and the French abandoned their plans only when the Finns concluded peace with the Russians.

Moscow, however, might have been somewhat influenced. Their amiable ambassador in Stockholm, Madame Kollontai, born in Finland, had rich experience and deep convictions. The daughter of a tsarist general, she had broken with her family, joined the socialist cause, and shared exile with the Bolshevik leaders. After the November revolution, she served as a people's commissar for social questions in Lenin's first government. Once arrested and expelled from Sweden as a socialist agitator, she returned there in 1930 as the envoy of the Soviet state. She now seemed to appreciate Swedish warnings that the wars in the east and in the west were in danger of being combined. Intervention by Western powers, perhaps with the aid of Sweden, would be highly unwelcome. The prospect that Germany would be drawn into such events and thus establish a foothold in the far North, close to Russia's borders, was not attractive. The way out was to compromise and engage Sweden in the peace process. The Russians came to insist on using the Swedish diplomatic channel to Helsinki and showed a sudden comprehension for Swedish interests in the Aland Islands. Moscow was eager to assure the Swedes, through a direct message from Molotov, that the rumors about Soviet interest in access to an Atlantic port was, as publicly stated, pure fabrication. To prove the point, the new and progressively harsher Soviet peace proposals did not include any territorial demands in the area of the Arctic Ocean but instead contained a promise to evacuate from Petsamo (except for part of the Rybachi Peninsula), an area sensitive to Sweden and Norway. Clearly, this was part of an effort to alienate the Swedes from the Finns, but at the same time Swedish interest in Finnish independence was recognized. Madame Kollontai was instructed to deny rumors of Soviet demands to include Kuusinen in the Finnish government and to state that "Moscow was fully aware that Sweden was particularly concerned about the internal liberty in Finland and will take all due regard thereto, being particularly concerned to maintain good relations with Sweden."

As it became more certain that Sweden would not itself intervene and would oppose Western intervention across its territory, Moscow became somewhat less ardent in its courtship. In any case, all through this time a flood of Swedish representations in Moscow to soften territorial demands on Finland had been consistently and totally unsuccessful. Moscow was thus prepared to cater to specifically Swedish interests but was unwilling to let Stockholm have any say on territorial issues between the U.S.S.R. and Finland. Moscow was also ready to take note of, if not in fact pay great attention to, Swedish sentiments on the internal set-up in Finland. Its exact position on these issues depended upon fluctuating international conditions and the use it could make of Sweden to further its own interests. It was clear that Swedish advice to the Helsinki government was tolerated only if it went in a direction favorable to the Soviet Union but that it would in itself normally be unwelcome.

Swedish-Finnish cooperation in a "neutral, defensive bloc" is a case where these strands of Soviet behavior can be studied. Up until the Winter War, the Russians could see no benefits whatsoever in such a scheme. As pro-German elements dominated Finnish politics, Moscow feared such cooperation would acquire a slant toward Berlin. Finland in itself was not seen as a threat but as an area of strategic interest where Swedish presence would only complicate Soviet plans. Paasikivi (p. 302) speculates that a Finnish-Swedish defense union in 1939 would have averted the Soviet attack. During the war, the Russians were obviously opposed to any defense cooperation between the two countries but were willing to soft-pedal objections to Swedish arms deliveries and volunteers, wishing to avoid even larger Swedish involvement and being aware of Swedish recommendations that Helsinki come to an agreement with Moscow.

After the Winter War, Moscow seemed to hesitate for a short while (Paasikivi, p. 295) but then decided not to tolerate any outsiders in its own sphere. Molotov thus expressed in detail to the Swedish ambassador in Moscow Soviet opposition to ideas of a defense union between Sweden, Norway, and Finland. Such plans, Molotov said, would violate Sweden's neutrality as well as Finland's peace treaty with the U.S.S.R. "If Sweden changed its neutral policy, the Soviet Union would also change its policy toward Sweden," declared Molotov. Arguments about the purely defensive and neutral character of the arrangement did not impress the Russian, nor did it occur to him that it might be in Soviet interests to have Finland tied to a neutral and prudent Sweden instead of looking to Germany to help it satisfy its revanchist frustrations.

Moscow had welcomed the German occupation of Norway and Denmark, not, presumably, because of any desire to see these two small states included in the Greater Reich but because the German invasion got Berlin deeper into the war and precluded any chance for accommodation with the British. Sweden was another matter. A move against that country would bring the Germans dangerously close to the Soviet sphere and get it further embroiled in Baltic affairs. It is thus not surprising that Molotov asked for a meeting with Schulenburg, the German ambassador to Moscow, about "rumors . . . that Germany would soon be forced to include Sweden in her Scandinavian operations," pointing out "that in his opinion Germany and definitely the Soviet Union were vitally interested in preserving Swedish neutrality." When this Soviet position was later repeated in the Berlin talks between Hitler and Molotov in November, the Soviet perspective had changed but the interests were the same. Now Swedish neutrality was seen as desirable in the context of a hypothetical Soviet-Finnish war.

The Russians, mostly for their own tactical reasons, seem to have wavered in the confidence they put in Swedish neutrality. Molotov pointed out in 1940 that "the present Swedish government is certainly neutral but there are other groups who support a war policy. Sandler (a former foreign minister) is a leader of such a group. . . . Sweden can get a new government at any time" (a surprising statement, given the set-up of the Swedish government) (Paasikivi). In talks with Hitler/ Ribbentrop, Molotov on the other hand seemed to pay little attention to Hitler's ideas that Sweden might join a war started by a renewed Russian attack on Finland. He clearly thought this was a transparently false argument designed to prevent the U.S.S.R. from exercising its domination over Finland, which had been given to it by the 1939 treaty.

Both Sweden and the Soviet Union had considerable interest in expanding trade relations. The Swedes were told in April

1940 by the skillful trade negotiator Anastas Mikoyan that they could buy attack aircraft and large quantities of oil and gasoline from the Soviet Union if they delivered ammunition and railway equipment, all on credit. When the Swedes eagerly responded to this offer--enticing to an economically isolated country surrounded by German armies--the Soviet promises were rapidly scaled down to much more modest proportions and linked to various airy schemes. The outcome of it all was a trade agreement which would not play a major role for any of the partners and which was soon superseded by military events.

BETWEEN THE WARS

Soon after the end of the Winter War, Germany in April 1940 occupied Norway and Denmark and moved into France, effectively neutralizing the Western powers in the Nordic area and alleviating Moscow's residual anxiety that somehow the capitalist states would, after all, settle without a full-scale war. For almost six months, until the Germans started to show their own active interest in Finland in early autumn 1940, Moscow could thus feel unhampered by other great powers in its dealings with Helsinki.

A series of new demands were now made, starting from June 1940. Most noteworthy was the Soviet stand as to the Aland Islands, where its great-power domination in the Baltic was stressed. The Aland fortifications had to be demolished and the U.S.S.R. allowed a large consulate there. Furthermore, the nickel mines in Petsamo should be brought under Russian control and transit rights given on Finnish trains to the Hango base. Rumors were rampant about Soviet troop concentrations on the Finnish-Soviet border. Internal Finnish politics came under Russian scrutiny and some politicians (Tanner) had to leave the government on Russian insistence. All this took place against the background of the occupation of the Baltic states and their conversion into Soviet republics in the summer of 1940. In part, the demands grew out of Soviet concern over revanchist feelings in Finland, repeated many times by Molotov to Paasikivi, now ambassador in Moscow, and the idea that the Finnish government "planned to exploit twists in the world war for its own benefit" and undo the peace treaty.   Trust was clearly lacking on both sides as to the intentions of the other party.

Molotov's way of explaining Soviet policy toward Finland in his talks with Hitler in November 1940 was clearly sinister: "The Finnish question was still unresolved."   The Soviet government considered it its duty to definitely settle the Finnish question; the old German-Russian agreement assigned Finland to the Russian sphere of influence.   "There must be neither German troops in Finland nor political demonstrations in that country against the Soviet-Russian Government." Hitler stressed that Germany did not desire any war in the Baltic Sea, had economic needs in Finland but was not politically interested, and only wanted to clarify whether Russia had the intention of going to war against Finland.   "Molotov answered his question somewhat evasively with the statement that everything would be all right if the Finnish government would give up its ambiguous attitude toward the U.S.S.R. and if the agitation against Russia among the population (slogans such as 'Nobody was a Finn who approved of the last Russo-Finnish Peace Treaty') would cease." Molotov later explained that there was no question of a war in the Baltic but of a settlement "on the same scale as in Bessarabia and in the adjacent countries."

Soviet actions and Molotov's statements show a determination in 1940-41 not to let Finland slip out of the Russian sphere, especially since revanchist trends were clearly apparent there.   Paasikivi expressed his view in a private letter from Moscow that "the military circles here were displeased that the Finnish war had been left unfinished and the intentions were to conquer Finland in its entirety soon after the annexation of the Baltic states" (Jagerskiold, p. 216). However, in view of German opposition, Moscow was apparently willing to forego armed force to secure its privileged position in Finland, as was made clear in Molotov's statement to Schulenburg (25 November) that the U.S.S.R. "undertakes to ensure peaceful relations with Finland."

THE NEW WAR

On 31 December 1940, the Finnish minister in Berlin expressed hope for his country during a visit to Ribbentrop's deputy. "In his homeland people were now reassured, because they thought they knew that in a future conflict with Russia they would not stand alone" (Sontag and Beddie, p. 264). Indeed, a new phase had come in Finnish-Soviet relations. In June 1941, German troops attacked from northern Finland "to secure the Petsamo region and its ore mines as well as the Arctic Ocean route and then to advance jointly with Finnish forces against the Murmansk railroad" (Hitler's directive of 18 December 1940 for Operation Barbarossa). Finland declared war after Russian planes bombed Helsinki.

Six months later, the territories given up in 1940 had been retaken and Finnish troops occupied large areas in East Karelia between Ladoga and Onega. The Soviet defense was weak; the best units had been concentrated against the German attack. Thereafter the Finns refused to move farther or to participate in the German siege of Leningrad. The front thus remained calm for three years until June 1944 when the Soviet grand offensive led the Russians over the Karelian Isthmus into Viborg. The Finns finally succeeded in thwarting the offensive. A few weeks later, when Russian troops had to be moved to the Central front against Germany, truce talks, which had started in March, resumed and were concluded in September.

The Soviet negotiating technique preceding the agreement was ingenious, splitting Helsinki from Berlin and intimating more favorable conditions than finally would be granted. In November 1943, Moscow told the Finns, via Sweden, that negotiations could start and that the U.S.S.R. "did not intend to incorporate Finland as a province of the Soviet Union or violate Finnish independence." When, after four months, Moscow's demands were communicated they corresponded fairly well (except for disposition of the Porkkala area) to what was finally decided. All along, a major precondition was that Finland, before any negotiations could start, must break relations with Germany and promise to intern (or, later, to expel) all German troops in Finland. As in 1939, the Russians underestimated Finnish stubbornness. The conditions proposed in March 1944 were refused. Stalin, who had already told the Allies in Teheran the approximate terms he had decided upon, was obviously unwilling to retreat and had made this abundantly clear by publishing the demands.

Thus, the first talks aborted and the Russians had to undertake their major offensive two months later. In September, when the Finnish negotiators returned, there were no margins for Soviet concession or even for discussion. Molotov, who might have been blamed for not having brought the Finns out of the war earlier, presented the Russian demands in a superior and peremptory fashion and requested an immediate Finnish answer. In a private discussion with Enckell, the Finnish delegation leader, he referred to the "bloody and criminal Finnish government" and promised a total occupation of Finland, already being prepared, if the Russian proposals were not accepted. In another private conversation, Molotov told Hackzell, the Finnish prime minister, that there were two schools of opinion on Finland among Soviet leaders: one group, in Leningrad, favored occupation and liquidation of Finland; the Moscow group favored an armistice which would allow Finland to continue as an independent country. After vain efforts to soften the terms, the Finns signed the truce.

The truce and the later peace treaty required Finland to recognize the treaty of 1940. The Porkkala area, 380 square kilometers to the southwest of Helsinki, was to be leased to the Soviet Union for fifty years. Petsamo in the north would be turned over to the U.S.S.R. Finland's armed forces were to be radically limited and $300 million were to be paid in war reparations. Finland agreed to cooperate with the Allies (in effect, the Soviet Union) in detaining and sentencing persons guilty of war crimes and in breaking up all organizations of a "fascist nature." An Allied Control Commission under Soviet leadership was set up to enforce the truce. Western political observers regarded these terms as lenient as they had expected Finland either to be absorbed by the U.S.S.R. or to become a satellite.

STALIN'S FINNISH POLICY

Why did Stalin conclude a peace treaty with Finland that did not secure total Soviet control, but only promised important influence?

Khrushchev comments: "Stalin showed statesmanly wisdom here. He knew that the territory of Finland wasn't relevant to the basic needs of the world proletarian revolution. When we signed a treaty just ending the war itself it was more profitable for us than an occupation would have been. Finland's cessation of hostilities set a good example for other satellites of Hitlerite Germany and it also made good marks for us with the Finnish people" (*Khrushchev Remembers*, Part I, p. 165). Indeed, political and military considerations combined in 1944. In the last phase of the war, all Russian troops had to be thrown against Germany to establish Soviet positions for the postwar political settlement. The Finns were obliged by the truce agreement to neutralize the German military threat--seven divisions strong--on Russia's long, secondary front. If the Soviets had demanded unconditional capitulation, they would have risked continued and desperate Finnish resistance.

The Finnish decision to turn decisively and quickly against their former allies, the Germans, and to force them out of Finland was both politically and militarily important. It showed will and determination to cooperate with the Russians and to break with Berlin. It made it possible to avoid the presence of Soviet troops as an occupying or "liberating" force in Finland, which would necessarily have changed the status of Finland in Moscow's eyes. "You extend your social system as far as your armies have reached," Stalin said to Djilas in 1945. Indeed, of all the countries on the European continent that had participated in the war, Finland was the only one to escape occupation. In Teheran, Stalin had outlined his plans for Finland and they did not include wholesale occupation. Churchill's and Roosevelt's intercessions on behalf of Finland were no doubt important but hardly decisive. The Western Allies had more important business to conduct and would not have forced the issue. Finland, having joined Germany in its aggression and having rejected Roosevelt's offers as late as early 1943 to mediate in Moscow, was not by any means as popular as it had been four years earlier. Russia, on the other hand, was winning its war against Germany with tremendous sacrifice.

In fact, the Russians treated the Finns better after the war than the U.S. and the U.K. had expected. If Stalin had refrained from pressing the Finnish issue in order to avoid Allied displeasure, he must also have considered the regional context. The U.S.S.R. would be the dominant power in the Baltic. It would not have to consider any important countervailing influence, as in Central Europe. Churchill asserted in Teheran that "Russia would end the war as the leading power in the Baltic." Russia could afford to exercise its influence indirectly. The positions acquired through the peace treaty could, if necessary, be used later to extend Soviet control. If circumstances in Finland permitted, a Communist government might later come to power. Now, the gain would be too small and the trouble too great to antagonize the Americans and the British by a too obvious and excessive territorial appetite.

The history of Stalin's dealings with the Finns suggests that decisive Soviet action to achieve direct control over Finland would have been taken only if Moscow's "reasonable" desire for influence had been faced with inflexible and inimical policies in Helsinki. Stalin must also have considered that the Finns, reacting to excessive pressure or force, would put up resistance which could only be overcome at considerable cost. The most important of the factors deciding Finland's fate might have been outside of Finnish control, but Finnish policies, fighting spirit, and internal unity tipped the balance.

THE SOVIET UNION AND SWEDEN, 1941-1945

Through most of the war, Moscow demonstrated understanding for the narrow margins of Swedish foreign policy and the necessity for Sweden to accede to some German demands. Such an attitude was, of course, to be expected from Hitler's ally, before the German attack on Russia. But even when concessions were made by Stockholm to enable German deliveries of war material to Finnish troops, Moscow made only perfunctory protests while stressing its interests in continued good relations. As feelers were put out in early 1942 to engage Stockholm in separate Soviet peace talks with Finland, Madame Kollontai underlined Soviet understanding that Sweden could not venture too far in such activity, so as not to risk Hitler's wrath and reprisals. The essential point for Moscow at this time was to keep Sweden out of the war, and it conducted relations with Stockholm accordingly.

As the fortunes of war began to turn in early 1943, however, the tone hardened. The Soviet message became that, in this new situation, Soviet interests must get higher priority in Sweden than German and Finnish ones, notwithstanding that the Baltic was still entirely under German control. Molotov even suggested to his Western Allies at the foreign ministers' conference in Moscow 1943 that Stockholm should be forced to permit the use of Swedish air bases by Allied aircraft operating against Germany. Swedish economic aid to Finland was now seen as helping to prolong Finland's war and thus, indirectly, as assistance to Germany. Soviet media started hinting at secret Swedish-German accords.

Soviet historians (e.g., Voronkov), presumably reflecting high-level attitudes even at that time, make a point that were it not for Soviet successes in the war in 1942-43, Sweden would have been occupied by Nazi Germany. Thus, the Soviets maintain, what saved the country was not, as the Swedes believe, its pragmatic neutrality and progressively mightier armed forces, but the Soviet capacity to fight and defeat Hitler's Germany.

Moscow made it clear in 1943 that it wanted to keep Sweden at a distance except as a technical channel in its dealings with Finland. Any ideas of a future Swedish-Finnish union or of a Nordic bloc that included Finland met with Soviet opposition. However, a neutral Scandinavian union that excluded Finland, to counterbalance Western influence in Norway and Denmark, was treated with some understanding by the Soviet Union.

The Finnish question, which had only recently produced positive Swedish contacts with Moscow, now seemed to present itself in a more logical context as a source of conflict. Of some importance, certainly, was Russian awareness of active Swedish lobbying on behalf of Finland in Western capitals, which bore fruit in the Allied discussions in Teheran. The Russians, however, continued to use the Swedish channel to Helsinki and expected and got Swedish pressure on the Finns to propose peace talks. When Moscow offered the first truce in March 1944, Sweden joined with the U.S. and Britain in advising acceptance. Nevertheless, the Russian leaders still seemed to doubt Swedish sincerity. It was only when Sweden's king publicly appealed to the Finns to accept the Russian conditions as a basis for negotiations that Soviet suspicions about Swedish policy evaporated--to such a degree that the Soviet government sent a special letter to thank the king for his major contribution to peace.

Chapter 2

TENSION, ACCOMMODATION, AND RESTRAINT: SOVIET-NORDIC POSTWAR RELATIONS UNTIL THE EARLY 1960s

POSTWAR INTERFERENCE IN FINLAND, 1945-1947

President Paasikivi was an astute observer of the Soviet policy makers and had the opportunity to study their behavior in more than fifty meetings with Stalin and Molotov. During his stay as ambassador to Moscow after the Winter War, he told his American counterpart that "he had learned that prestige meant more to them than anything else; that their invariable policy was to obtain what they could for as little as possible and then ask for more; that they never sacrificed immediate gains for considerations for the future; that they paid no attention to what was said, but only to what was done; that they endeavored to be paid a high price for what they must do anyway; and that they were impervious to ethical and humanitarian factors or those of abstract justice, being influenced exclusively by practical and realistic considerations" (U.S. Department of State, *Foreign Relations of the United States* (FR), 1941, vol. 1, p. 30; and Paasikivi, p. 35).

The pessimistic and moody ambassador of 1941, who had sometimes used even harsher words to describe his own government, had to deal after World War II first as prime minister and later as president of the republic with a predominant Soviet presence in his own country. The Allied

Control Commission went about its work without undue magnanimity. It was dominated by the Russians, and the British played only a minor role, acting on the basis of Foreign Minister Eden's instructions of 9 August 1944: "Although we shall no doubt hope that Finland be left some real degree of at least cultural and commercial independence and parliamentary regime, Russian influence will in any event be predominant in Finland and we shall not be able, nor would it serve any important British interest, to contest that influence."

Zhdanov, chairman of the Control Commission, and his superior in Moscow wanted to show that the U.S.S.R. had the ultimate authority to decide Finland's fate, but so far there was no evidence of Soviet intention to radically change Finnish political institutions and practices. The cautious, cooperative, but stubborn attitudes of Finnish leaders, particularly Paasikivi, reduced the scope of activity and the demands of the Control Commission. The Finns acted as though Moscow had only limited security interests in Finland, canonized this principle in all their rhetoric, and seemed to get it accepted by the Soviets.

The ACC thus voluntarily abandoned some of its prerogatives and passed up numerous opportunities to precipitate a crisis and increase its control over Finland. Although Soviet pressure caused Finnish law to be superseded and eight Finnish leaders were given prison sentences for their wartime activities, a general witch-hunt was never forced through. New political leaders emerged, but they were elected by the Finns, not imposed by the Russians. The discovery of arms caches was used by the Russians as justification for more Soviet interference, but no control over the military was established or attempted. Heavy war reparations were exacted, but the Soviets agreed to an extension of the payment schedule in order to ease the burden. The local Communists were encouraged to partici-pate in the government and did so. The Soviet ratification of the Paris peace agreement in 1947 was accompanied by a series of good-will gestures, including passage of Finnish trains through the Porkkala area, albeit with the windows closed ("the longest train tunnel in Finland"). But East-West tension was already growing, creating risks for Finland.

THE SOVIET-FINNISH PACT OF FRIENDSHIP, COOPERATION, AND MUTUAL ASSISTANCE

Both the Finns and the Russians saw advantages in a pact of mutual assistance and friendship when the matter was first brought up by Zhdanov in 1944-45. Not surprisingly, perspectives differed. Some Finns, particularly the military, had hopes that, if Moscow's interest in Finland was mainly defensive and military, a treaty confirming Soviet confidence in Helsinki and establishing limited military cooperation between Finland and the U.S.S.R. could be exchanged for border adjustments (Porkkala and the Saima channel) plus the right of Finland to maintain a reasonably large defense force. Mannerheim, who was president until March 1946, endorsed these views. He proposed a draft treaty which included a provision that, in the event of "aggression against Finland, against the U.S.S.R. through Finland, or against both states, the two parties agree to aid each other with all available means on Finnish territory, in the Northern Baltic, and in the Finnish Gulf." Mannerheim thus went somewhat further than the treaty which was concluded three years later in not restricting mutual defense to Finnish territory exclusively and in making Soviet military action slightly more automatic in case of "aggression" in the area. However, nothing was said in his draft about consultations in case of outside threats, a topic which later came to assume importance.

Paasikivi and Foreign Minister Enckell were interested in the treaty as a step toward lasting peace with the Russians, thereby ridding Finland of the humiliating presence and domination of the Control Commission and perhaps making possible the other benefits envisaged by the military. Finland had nothing to lose, they reasoned, since, in the event of a European war, Russia would consider occupying Finland anyway, but would be rather less interested in doing so if the two countries had concluded a treaty of cooperation by which Finland demonstrated its will to defend itself against the West, "the Anglo-Americans."

Russian interest in a mutual assistance pact waned, however, even though they had first broached the subject. Zhdanov told Paasikivi in 1946 that Moscow preferred to conclude a peace treaty as a first step. Perhaps other matters were more urgent for Moscow--the status of Poland, Hungary, *et al.*, was still to be settled. Perhaps, too, Moscow expected that the internal situation in Finland might evolve favorably, with the Communists playing a larger role.

A few years later, however, the international situation had changed drastically. In 1945-47, local Communists under Russian supervision took power in Poland, Hungary, Rumania, and Bulgaria. Several reasons explain why the "Finnish pattern" was not followed in these countries. Soviet troops had occupied all of them; Allied wartime understandings had put them in the Soviet sphere of interest; their geographic position made them strategically more important than Finland; Western reaction to the takeovers was too weak to change Stalin's mind but strong enough to keep his suspicions alive; and Soviet dominance had to be assured by direct fiats, since local Communists were unable to establish and maintain control by themselves.

The Soviets feared that restored prosperity in the West might become attractive to the not yet fully secured Soviet satellites. The ideas behind the Marshall plan were obvious: "Under the restoration of the economy . . . the imperialist circles of the United States openly understood the return to a situation where the world capitalist economic system would recover hegemony and the socialist area would first be pushed back to its frontiers of 1939 and then fully liquidated" (Mileikovski, as cited in Ulam, p. 436). Thus, the American "containment policy," starting with the Marshall plan and followed by the creation of NATO, was magnified by the Russians into a "roll-back" scheme. The Western interpretation was that Moscow disliked the American aid program because it strengthened both European and American economies and thus bolstered defense against Communist advances.

Whatever Stalin's exact thinking, he found it necessary to more firmly, but prudently, establish a secure order along the western frontiers of the U.S.S.R., since he felt pressure would increase on the Soviet Union to surrender some of her wartime gains. The Nordic area was no exception. Secret defense talks among Scandinavian military forces was an example of dangerous developments in this region.

In February 1948, Stalin wrote to Paasikivi suggesting talks about a treaty between Finland and the U.S.S.R. "on the same basis as those recently concluded between the U.S.S.R. and Hungary and Rumania, respectively, neighbors of the Soviet Union having fought against the U.S.S.R. on the side of Germany." The reaction in Finland was violent. Was this to be a replay of 1939? Would the Soviets try to treat Finland as they had treated the Eastern European countries? Had not Zhdanov only a few months earlier (in a speech at the first meeting of Cominform in September 1947) lumped Finland together with Rumania and Hungary in the "anti-fascist camp" as a "new democracy"? And had not Hertta Kuusinen, leader of the Communists in parliament and daughter of one of Stalin's advisers, claimed that "Finland must follow the road taken by these countries"? Mannerheim and Paasikivi talked gloomily in private about the likelihood of Finland becoming a Soviet satellite, or even, in due time, being incorporated into the Soviet Union. A considerable body of opinion developed advocating outright refusal of Stalin's proposal and accepting the probability that this would lead to Soviet military action. The Swedish press echoed the doomsday prophecies, but the government in Stockholm, reasserting Sweden's neutrality, abstained from any comments on the situation.

Prudence prevailed in Helsinki over demonstrative gesticulation. Stalin's invitation was accepted but the Finnish delegation was given firm and restrictive instructions. Finland could certainly agree to a treaty with some military content. It was its sovereign duty to resist aggression on its territory, whether in self-defense or in defense of an attack against the Soviet Union. It could state its right to demand Soviet aid in a defensive struggle and to consult with Moscow in case of a threat to its territory. The difficult questions were whether

Finnish forces should be used outside Finnish territory and
whether Soviet military aid would be given without an explicit
Finnish request (as in the Eastern European treaties), and who
should decide if the danger was such that consultations were
required between Helsinki and Moscow. If the treaty contained
a provision for a permanent consultation machinery to align the
foreign policy stands of the two capitals, Finland would acquire
semi-satellite status.

The mood in the Finnish delegation was somber as it set
out, on 20 March 1948, under the leadership of Prime Minister
Pekkala and two foreign ministers who both had long experience
from official duty in St. Petersburg. Another member of the
delegation was Yrjo Leino, a Communist, albeit, as it turned
out, a renegade one.

Moscow's Finnish Considerations

With hindsight we can perhaps make some guesses about
discussions taking place in Moscow at this time on the Finnish
question. Zhdanov's Cominform statement is quoted above. He
is also on record as stating in a conversation with Djilas in
January 1948 that "It was a mistake that we did not occupy
Finland." (In a later Djilas version, Stalin agreed, adding that
"we took too much account of the Americans--they wouldn't
have lifted a finger anyway." No explanation is given why this,
the most important part of the conversation, was omitted by
Djilas in his earlier book.) Loose after-dinner talk of this kind
should not be given too much weight and its purpose in being
spoken to a Yugoslav visitor in 1948 must be suspect. The
context of the remarks is also noteworthy. Zhdanov made his
remark as a follow-up to high praise of Finnish war reparation
deliveries. It almost seemed as if Zhdanov, whose experience
included running a large industrial region in Russia, longed for

an infusion of the efficiency of the Finns and the high quality of their economy into his more backward system.

The Leningrad party chief, who in 1936 had warned Finland not to get "entangled in big adventures," had acquired a bad name in Finland, as did many of his successors in that city. Finnish perceptions of Zhdanov were further sharpened by his reputation as the executioner of Estonian independence in 1940. In Helsinki, however, he gradually gained a somewhat better reputation as head of the Allied Control Commission. Finnish negotiators who met him in Moscow were struck by his positive interest in Finnish economic problems and his good relations with bourgeois politicians (Soderhjelm, p. 167f.). That impression might have been misleading indeed, since Zhdanov's main task now was to mobilize the resources of international communism for the subversion of Western Europe. Zhdanov's position in the Soviet hierarchy had become somewhat uncertain by this time. The preeminence he seemed to have had over Malenkov, Beria, *et al.*, was slipping away, and ended with his untimely and mysterious death shortly thereafter.

Whatever ideas Zhdanov or others might have had (Mikoyan was referred to by his colleagues as "Finland's advocate"), it was Stalin who made the decisions. He knew the stubborn Finns and understood that they would resist ultimata. In 1945 he might have envisaged a take-over in Helsinki via a strong Communist party, but by 1948 that possibility was remote. A coup may have been contemplated but, if it was, the idea was abandoned. Evidence of such deliberations, which are hidden from outsiders, is slim.

The Communists were in fact represented in various Finnish governments up to July 1948 but always as a minority. Yrjo Leino was appointed interior minister in 1945 and set out to place Communists in important positions in the police. However, he and his colleagues failed to muster support for their party, whose influence was slipping after having risen in the first two postwar years.

Some accounts relate plans for a coup in early 1948, but they are not corroborated. There is speculation that Stalin proposed his treaty in the belief that the Finns would refuse. Internal unrest would then have been fomented by the Communists, followed by intervention by Soviet troops. Leino himself, however, had fallen out of favor with Moscow well before that time, and he relates in his memoirs (unpublished) that he was asked by Molotov and Zhdanov in the autumn of 1947 to resign his post but did not obey. Another defected Communist (Tuominen) claims that Leino, by revealing the coup plans to the Finnish commander-in-chief, aborted the project. This murky story is made no more transparent by eager denials from Hertta Kuusinen, Leino's divorced wife, who was later married to Ture Lehen, Comintern's specialist on armed coups.

In the spring of 1948, the international situation dictated against an open Soviet conflict with Helsinki which would have to be settled by force. The Communist coup in Czechoslovakia at the end of February, which occurred between the date of Stalin's letter to Helsinki and the arrival of the Finnish delegation to Moscow two months later, had alerted the already irate Westerners. Yugoslav nationalism was proving that Communists in power could be even more obnoxious than prudent bourgeois politicans, and the simmering conflict in that country might require forceful action. The situation in Germany, particularly in Berlin, was becoming more intense and culminated in the summer of 1948 in the Berlin blockade. The Western Europeans were establishing a military alliance under the Brussels Treaty and had initiated discussions with the United States about Atlantic cooperation, which could have implications for the Scandinavian countries, including Sweden. Soviet military moves or threats against Finland during this period could have adverse effects in the Nordic countries and lead to a sharpening of already dangerous tensions in exchange for only modest benefits. Once again, Stalin's priorities dictated a benevolent attitude toward the Finns. International tension, concentrated on Europe, made a settlement with Finland desirable.

However, Moscow also had good reason not to delay solidifying and formalizing its relationship with Finland. Soviet control there was reduced once the ACC had left Finland, but the U.S.S.R. could hardly criticize Finnish behavior: "fascist organizations" had been scrupulously suppressed; Marshall plan aid had been refused (after clear signals from Moscow and with more circumspection than the Czechs had shown); and Helsinki kept clear of any grouping of states that could be seen to have an anti-Soviet tendency. Suspicions in Moscow were nurtured, however, by a lively debate in the Finnish press about the Marshall plan decision, by the grant of some American credits to encourage trade with the West (although the credits were given most discreetly), and by Finland's entry into such strongholds of capitalism as the IMF and the World Bank. The Swedish press, more outspoken than the self-restrained Finnish press, did not make things any easier with its cold-war rhetoric about the Soviet Union.

Treaty Negotiations

The Finnish delegation was received in Moscow by Molotov. With his most pleasant and forthcoming manners, he managed to calm the nervous Finns. The Soviet official, whose mind must have been full of other concerns, such as the Berlin blockade, the impending Communist take-over in China, and schemes to unseat the renegade Tito, to mention but a few of the most pressing matters of the time, no doubt viewed these talks with the Finns as a pleasant interlude.

In the very first meeting, the Russians, while repeating the proposal to use the Hungarian/Rumanian treaty as a point of departure, agreed to work on the basis of a Finnish draft. Two issues soon became prominent. The first concerned the explicit stipulation in the Finnish draft that Soviet military aid should be given to Finland only with Finland's agreement and after it had become apparent that Finland's own forces were unable to meet the aggression. The Russians proposed instead that any such aggression should be met "jointly" by Finnish and Soviet forces, which meant that Soviet aid would be sent in at an early phase of the conflict and that it would be automatic, without prior agreement or negotiations between Helsinki and Moscow. Molotov pointed out that the Soviet proposal on this point was still much more restrictive than the terms of the Hungarian/ Rumanian treaty and that certain earlier statements by Paasikivi went as far.

The second issue concerned the threat of aggression. The Finns had proposed that the parties "consult in case a threat of a military aggression is being noted," i.e., noted by both parties. The Russians used somewhat more nebulous wording which was linked directly to the actual aggression mentioned in the first paragraph and referred to "measures to be taken to obviate the threat of such aggression." The Russian wording could in fact be interpreted as referring only to measures to be taken when war had already broken out, whereas the Finnish text, as Molotov later pointed out, clearly referred to consultations in peacetime about an outside threat.

The Finns countered with a compromise to the first paragraph which made clear Finland's duty to defend itself "if need be with the assistance and jointly with the U.S.S.R.," the actual details of such assistance "to be agreed by both parties." Thus, Soviet participation in Finland's defense would neither come necessarily very early nor be in any way automatic. The Finnish draft was accepted right away, as was Helsinki's original proposal on consultations in case of a threat, which indeed from Moscow's point of view might have been better than its own proposal.

The preambular paragraphs mentioned "Finland's desire to keep apart from conflicts of interest between the Great Powers," a statement of Finnish neutrality. Indeed, if the Soviet Union were to be attacked through any other quarter than through Finnish territory--land, sea, or air--Finland retained its full right to remain neutral. The treaty also reaffirmed that "both parties undertook not to participate in alliances or coalitions directed against the other party."

The Russians thus showed remarkable and unusual flexibility, abandoning at the outset Stalin's suggestion in his letter to Paasikivi for a treaty analogous to the Hungarian/ Rumanian one and agreeing to amend considerably their own proposed changes to the original Finnish draft. No wonder that the local Finnish Communists were left somewhat out in the cold by arguing up to the last moment for a treaty along the original Stalinist lines.

The Finns were understandably relieved. The treaty did not restrict Finnish independence any more than recent history, geography, and relationships of strength had done already. The Russians likewise seemed pleased. Stalin exuded good will and satisfaction in his short speech at the signature ceremony. In words that were to be repeated many times down to the present day, the treaty was hailed as a decisive turning point in Soviet-Finnish relations, which would in the future be imbued with friendship and mutual confidence, provided of course that much work and struggle was devoted to this cause. The former "lack of confidence" (nedoverie) was indeed contrasted to the present "confidence" (doverie) no less than twelve times. It "should be well understood by everyone *both* in Finland and in the Soviet Union" that a new era had now come. Stalin particularly stressed the Soviet attitude, unique among big powers, to respect in full the equality of all states, be they small or large, and to seek fruitful cooperation, as was so well symbolized by this treaty.

Indeed, the Treaty on Friendship, Cooperation, and Mutual Assistance (FCMA) seemed to broaden Finnish political margins. After the Communists were defeated in the parliamentary elections of July 1948, a purely Social Democratic government, from which the Communists were excluded, was formed. Finnish-Soviet relations suffered but remained cordial at the official level, as demonstrated a few months later in a major trade agreement. At the same time, however, frequent virulent criticism appeared in the Soviet press against the new government, "the men of 1939, reactionary forces trying to lead Finland into catastrophic and senseless adventures."

Soviet pressure on Finland, and on other Nordic countries in reference to Finland, in fact intensified after the treaty ceremonies in Moscow. The Finns were accused by Soviet media of harboring plans to join a Scandinavian defense alliance. When that scheme failed, Helsinki was accused of trying to establish links with the Western partners in the future Atlantic pact. Numerous protests were lodged by the Soviet ambassador concerning various anti-Soviet facets of Finnish society. Early in 1949, rumors were published about a concentration of Soviet troops along the Finnish border and about military exercises being held close to this border. Hints were made that the U.S.S.R. would be obliged to change its policy toward Finland if Sweden joined NATO. Such direct military and political actions may have been intended more as pressure on Norway and Sweden to abstain from membership in the Atlantic pact than as threats to Finland.

All during this period, Washington maintained the position it had held since the war: a prudent support of Finland's independence through limited financial and trade measures, taking great care not to awaken in Moscow suspicions of undue interference.

MOSCOW AND THE SCANDINAVIANS IN THE AFTERMATH OF THE WAR, 1945-1947

Scandinavia as a whole was seen in both Moscow and Washington as a neutral region leaning somewhat toward the West but with no firm links with any great power. All three Scandinavian countries tried to maintain good relations with the Soviet Union. Such an attitude was understandable. The Soviet Union, absent from the Baltic since 1918, now returned as the dominant power there. There was no other great power in the area to balance its influence. This colossal neighbor and its ruler were relatively unknown in the Scandinavian capitals. Apprehension in the face of this giant was mixed with admiration for its achievements. Russian armies had defeated Nazi Germany, and the people of the Soviet Union had suffered immensely to gain this victory. Old socialists, now in power in

Scandinavia, were certainly enemies of communism but all the same were full of respect for this historic accomplishment.

The Russians had an advantageous political and military position in the North. Throughout World War II and up to the 1950s, the primary source of Soviet security concerns in the Nordic region was in the perceived threat to the Leningrad heartland. The balance of forces in the Baltic and access to and exit from this area were major problems for Moscow. In the war the German navy had proven to be superior in the competition for mastery of these waters. After the war, however, the U.S.S.R. was by far the dominant power in the Baltic area. The general thrust of Soviet policy then came to be to convert the Baltic into a *mare clausum*, where only military vessels from the riparian states would be allowed and where these states would jointly exercise control over exit and entry. In the far North, Soviet troops had moved into northern Norway, liberating it from German troops. In that region, no other military force could balance the Soviet presence.

From the Nordic perspective, Russian military might was awesome but was exercised with some restraint. Moscow had negotiated a truce and later a peace with Finland.

Territories occupied by the Germans and liberated by Soviet forces (northern Norway and Bornholm) were soon handed back to Norway and Denmark. In both cases, there had been apprehensions that a price would have to be paid for Soviet withdrawal.

Each Scandinavian country had unique concerns and a special historical background in its relationship with the Soviet Union.

Sweden had to consider the new situation in the Baltic region. At the end of the war, Sweden had been subjected to considerable attacks in the Soviet press as having been too prone to cooperate with the Germans. These attacks were continued all through 1945, but somewhat abated in 1946.

Concurrently, Swedish media evolved in the opposite direction toward a progressively more critical view of the Soviet Union. In 1946, Stockholm extended a major commercial credit to the U.S.S.R., partly for political reasons and partly for, as it turned out mistaken, economic reasons. A postwar crisis in the West, it was believed, could be counterbalanced by access to the immense potential market in the East. The heated internal debate about this issue probably lessened its good-will value. Soviet media thus maintained a fairly suspicious attitude toward Sweden. Clearly, however, distinctions were now made between "anti-Soviet reactionaries" in the opposition and the government, principally Foreign Minister Unden, who took a more objective and balanced view. This distinction came in handy as the Stockholm government became subjected to virulent Swedish media attacks for its decision to return to the Soviet Union a contingent of Balts in German uniforms who had sought refuge from approaching Russian armies. All through the war, some 35,000 civilians from the Baltic countries had fled to Sweden from Russian or German occupation. As Germany collapsed, a sizeable number of Balts who had served in the German army came to Sweden. Those who were in uniform were sent back to the Allied powers, some 170 of them to the Soviet Union on the demand of the Soviet government.

Denmark sought political and commercial cooperation with the U.S.S.R., which was now, after all, the principal power in the Baltic, a fact that was consistently emphasized by Soviet officials in their contacts with Danish diplomats in Moscow. Dekanozov, a vice foreign minister, thus pointed out that "Denmark after this war is Russia's neighbor, direct neighbor, and we have no more competitors in the Baltic--a fact which Denmark should remember" (quoted in Bent Jensen, *Bidrag till oststatsforskningen*, 1983, vol. 4, p. 103).

Soviet forces had occupied Bornholm, a large Danish island in the Baltic east of the demarcation line which separated the east and west military zones in Germany. The Soviets withdrew in March-April 1946, however, having shown no desire to remain permanently on the island. The Soviet government expressed in a note to the Danish government its willingness to withdraw, "provided the Danish government is able to send its own troops to take control of the island and to establish Danish administration there without any foreign participation." Moscow has since used this note, whose contents were accepted by Denmark, to claim that no foreign troops should ever be allowed on the island. No basis exists in the text for this claim, however, since the only issue addressed by the note was the immediate take-over. This notwithstanding, the Danish government has exercised restraint in regard to foreign military presence on Bornholm.

At the council of foreign ministers meeting in Moscow in December 1945, Molotov expressed an interest in the status of the entrances to the Baltic Sea. Some Western apprehension arose that the Russians would use their military position on Bornholm to effect a political change as to the straits. No such moves were ever made by Moscow. The Russians thus did not repeat their wartime proposals to Germany to have an arrangement, like the Danube Commission, giving the U.S.S.R. a part in decisions concerning the Baltic Straits, but seemed content with Western assertions that the waterways should be open and free to all nations entering or leaving the Baltic. Moscow's new possessions on the eastern coast of the Baltic, such as Kaliningrad, also made further strongholds in this area militarily less interesting.

Soviet maritime forces in this area were continually strengthened and naval port facilities were expanded, while the twelve-mile limit, not yet customary in Europe, was declared for Soviet sea territory. The Baltic, however, did not become a diplomatic problem for the Soviets until the accession of Denmark to the Atlantic treaty and the realization of plans for a rearmament of Germany.

Moscow showed greater but still relatively subdued interest in the far North. *Norway* came out of the war with ambitions to play a bridge-building, conciliatory role as a neutral in world affairs. Initially, however, it had some thorny bilateral problems to settle with the U.S.S.R.

In the late 1950s, after the advent of submarine-based nuclear weapons, the Murmansk base complex gradually emerged as the single most vital strategic nerve center in the U.S.S.R., and great attention came to be given to northern Norway, Svalbard, and the Kola exit. Soviet concern, however, also marked the immediate postwar era. Transport routes to Murmansk had been crucial during the war; American positions on Greenland and Iceland demonstrated the strategic value of positions in the North Atlantic; and Russia had a traditional interest in this region. Molotov, speaking to Norway's Foreign Minister Lie in December 1944, requested that Norway give up its sovereignty over Svalbard and Bear Island. Molotov proposed that Svalbard be put under joint Norwegian-Soviet administration, and that Bear Island be transferred outright to the Soviet Union. The Soviet foreign minister was frank: "The Dardanelles--here we are locked in. Oresund--here we are locked in. Only in the north is there an opening, but this war has shown that the supply line to northern Russia can be cut or interfered with. This must not be repeated in the future. We have invested much in this part of the Soviet Union and it is so important for the entire Union's existence that we shall in the future ensure that northern Russia is permitted to live in security and peace" (Lie). Two years later, Molotov returned to the subject, which had been stalled by the Norwegians, and pointedly reminded Oslo that the two countries now shared a common border.

Before the 1920 treaty, Bear Island had indeed been Russian and Svalbard was no-man's land. However, the Soviet Union had accepted the treaty in 1935 without any reservations. Now it wanted to go back on its word. It could refer to wartime discussions in which the Norwegians had declared their readiness to negotiate an arrangement for the common defense of the island while retaining Norwegian sovereignty. These discussions, however, had taken place in the final, intense phase of the war when Russian troops advanced into northern Norway and when the safety of transport routes to Murmansk was of utmost importance to the Allies. Now the war had come to an end, and the Norwegians were unwilling to enter into a bilateral defense relationship with the U.S.S.R.

Washington at this time might have been ready to make a deal and allow Moscow to have bases on Spitzbergen so long as the Soviets raised no objections to American bases on Iceland and Greenland and no demands were made on Norwegian territory. When the issue became public in late 1946, however, most signatories to the Svalbard treaty objected to changes in the status of the island. Oslo shelved the matter for a while, strongly stressing to the Russians its nonaligned and friendly policies.

In 1947, Norway rejected the Soviet proposals, mainly because joint administration of the island would cause considerable problems in crises or war situations. Moscow did not press its demands but remained actively suspicious of any move to use the islands for military purposes.

The Russians were unaware that internal American discussions probably went further in the direction of Soviet interests than Moscow itself could have hoped for. The Soviets saw Norway and Denmark all through the war as an area of British-American military responsibility. Stalin, talking about postwar Europe in 1941, offered Foreign Secretary Eden British bases in Norway and Denmark in exchange for U.K. acquiescence in the siting of Soviet bases in Finland and Rumania and guarantees for the Baltic exits. The growth of Soviet power and prestige did not appreciably change this attitude, although Moscow obviously wished to see all Scandinavian countries adopt a neutral position.

At the end of the war, as Russian forces moved into Finnmark in northeastern Norway, harrassing German troops there, some Western concern was expressed "that they not permanently occupy Norwegian territory, in view of the potential threat to North Atlantic trade routes, Iceland and the northern approaches to the North Sea" (Joint Chiefs of Staff memorandum, September 1944, quoted in Lundestad, p. 38). Possession of the area westward to Lyngen would treble the Soviet ice-free coastline in the north and provide innumerable good harbors. American officials also feared that the Russians, given the proximity of this area to Murmansk, "will seek a pact

with Norway which will provide for Norwegian/Soviet defense
of northern Norway against any third power."

   If it had pursued the Germans further, the U.S.S.R. could
have claimed that, as the liberator of Norway, it was entitled to
a larger say in Allied affairs there. Because Stalin decided
against this course of action, he thus conceded Norway as an
area of predominantly Western influence. No doubt he expected
in return a similar British and American attitude regarding his
own sphere of influence in Eastern Europe. However, in direct
dealings with the Norwegians, Moscow dissuaded them from
allowing any foreign presence in the country, particularly in the
eastern part of northern Norway. Oslo was given to understand
that it also needed good relations with the U.S.S.R., a power that
now had important Altantic interests.

REALIGNMENT IN THE NORTH

After the war, tensions soon emerged between the victors. The
Scandinavians, true to their traditions and following a natural
course for small countries on the periphery of the European
continent, tried to ease the tensions without becoming directly
involved in the conflict. The votes cast in the U.N. by the three
countries demonstrated their desire to steer an independent
course between East and West. They came to be seen, at least in
Washington, as obstacles to the creation of a strong Western
European organization based on the Marshall plan. In varying
degrees, they were hesitant to align themselves with a Western
organization that was being heavily criticized by Moscow. Their
efforts were also aimed at bridging the gap between East and
West by trying to create links to the United Nations. In the
end, they decided to adhere to the Marshall plan while trying to
dilute its political content and limit American influence over the
economic policies of member countries. From the Soviet

perspective, this was a well-meaning but "politically naive" position.

As demands for loyalty increased from both sides, Scandinavian neutrality was viewed with growing suspicion in both Moscow and Washington. The idea of two opposing camps had become accepted in both capitals. Under pressure, the Scandinavians leaned somewhat toward the West, which further increased Soviet suspicions. Norway and Denmark, however, soon parted company with the Swedes over security policy.

Scandinavia was especially interesting to military planners. The British Chiefs of Staff, in a June 1947 report to the Foreign Office on the military importance of Scandinavia to the West, stated that, during the initial stages of a potential war with the Soviet Union, maintaining the integrity of that region would be almost as important as keeping France, Belgium, and Holland out of reach of the enemy. The report emphasized the industrial and raw material resources of the Scandinavian countries, the advantageous attack routes open to the Soviet Union via the Danish straits and the Norwegian coast, and the significance of Scandinavia for the enemy's defense: should the Soviet Union succeed in deploying its own air defense system there, it would be able to cut the direct air routes from North America to western Russia.

If, on the other hand, the Scandinavian countries could be made to join the West, they would offer it valuable raw materials and manpower. Second, they could provide bases from which air and naval operations could be directed to the northern waters and the Baltic Sea, and, because the region was "halfway to Moscow," it would also offer initial positions for rocket attacks and air raids aimed at disrupting communications between Russia and Western Europe should the Soviet army invade the West. Third, the Western powers would have the opportunity to deploy their own air defense system there. The strategic importance of Scandinavia was enhanced by the fact that air units deployed there would have a decisive effect in slowing down an attack launched from the East against Western Europe (Nevakivi in *Cooperation and Conflict*, 1984, p. 167).

A Scandinavian Defense Union: Norway,
Denmark, and NATO

As the world situation grew more tense, the main issue for
Moscow became what attitude to take toward the question of a
Scandinavian defense union. In 1947, Western powers were
inclined to encourage defense coordination among Sweden,
Norway, and Denmark, believing that, even if they did not
become tied to a Western European bloc, such cooperation would
strengthen these three countries vis-a-vis the Soviet Union. The
underlying assumption was also that the Scandinavians would
gravitate toward the West, as both the Danes and the
Norwegians were apt to do. The Western governments changed
their position in 1948, however, preferring to integrate Norway
and Denmark (and possibly, though less importantly, Sweden)
into the nascent North Atlantic grouping, and thereby block
Swedish efforts to recruit the two other Scandinavian countries
into an independent military community, which would have to
be neutral.

Nordic attitudes in early 1948 were marked by alarmist
perceptions of international events. The coup in Czechoslovakia,
the Berlin blockade, Stalin's ominous invitation to Paasikivi in
February 1948, rumors, mainly from American sources but
surprisingly not immediately and explicitly denied in Moscow,
that Norway would be approached with a similar request--
everything combined to create a war-scare in the North. The
Americans sent a naval task force to Norway to counteract
anticipated Soviet pressures. When Denmark sought arms from
the United States during the Berlin blockade and seemed to be
drawing closer to the West, Soviet naval and air forces were said
to have repeatedly violated Danish territory in the area of the
island of Bornholm.

The American military told the Scandinavians in mid-
March 1948 that they should either form their own defense
union or join the Western bloc to avoid being swallowed up, one
by one, by the Soviets. The Russian military, via *Krasnaya
Zvezda*, accused the Danes and Norwegians of already having

put their armed forces under the control of the United States and Great Britain, echoing local Communist propaganda. Sweden did not fare any better in the Soviet press. Swedish military investments, purchases of British Vampire aircraft, the extension of military airports, etc., were said to be evidence of a secret military pact between the Scandinavians and the Anglo-Americans.

The Norwegians and the Danes felt the need to seek security within a wider framework. The Swedes had a somewhat more sanguine view of Soviet intentions. War might come about, not through any purposeful Soviet decision to aggress, but rather by accident or as a result of defensive action. All the more reason to maintain a neutral buffer in the North.

At this time, Sweden was a considerable military power, at least in terms of its air force, which was matched in Western Europe only by the British. Norway and Denmark had no such military resources. Sensing the possibility of a split among the Nordic countries, Stockholm proposed a Scandinavian defense union independent of the power blocs. Such nonalignment was a must for Sweden, whose policy of neutrality was solidly anchored in its history and in the public opinion of the country.

A skeptical partisan description of Swedish thinking was given by the American ambassador in Stockholm in what he called "twelve fallacies" (Ambassador Matthew to the Secretary of State, 16 February 1948):

> Sweden may well keep out of a third war if it comes. Both sides may find Sweden's neutrality advantageous.

> Therefore, Sweden must take no step now which might lessen its chances of avoiding future war.

> Any steps toward the Westin political or military fields now will incur future Soviet ire and suspicion and therefore lessen Sweden's chances of avoiding involvement in a war. Present political neutrality may keep Sweden out.

If there is no war and the great powers compose their future differences, Sweden will be left in isolation to incur Soviet reprisals for any present leaning toward the West. (Look what great-power "deals" did to Czechoslovakia and Poland in 1939.)

In the last weeks before a war, Sweden will have ample opportunity to determine its policy, i.e., to side with the West or neutrality. Therefore, the time is not ripe to choose now.

Sweden's association with the West now may bring disastrous Soviet occupation of the kindred buffer state of Finland.

Any possible moral obligation to join other free nations to use moral influence to oppose Soviet expansion is subordinate to Swedish self-preservation through neutrality.

The moral influence of world opinion does not change Soviet policies anyway.

There is no danger that the West will resent Swedish neutrality and therefore leave Sweden to her fate. It is the devil (Russia) that must be appeased.

Because of its geographical position, Sweden is more vulnerable than Western Europe, i.e., a Maginot-line psychology in reverse without conception of modern warfare.

Even if "neutrality" is not the wisest policy, there must be no agitation against it for this would split the Swedish nation and internal unity in these times must be preserved at all cost.

The Eastern bloc stands for communism; the Western bloc may be dominated by "capitalist reaction." Sweden (Social Democratic majority) must pursue a middle course.

Strong Western pressure combined with clear threats was brought to bear on Sweden to abandon neutrality and join NATO. Stark scenarios were painted. The Soviet Union was the great threat to the Western world and neutrals would not be allowed, as they were in the last war, to sit on the fence, delivering goods and profiting from trade with both parties. The West would forcibly prevent any such commerce and the Russians would consequently find themselves obliged to occupy a country like Sweden to get what they wanted. In such a case, no neutral could count on Western help. In peacetime, likewise, military equipment would be sent first and perhaps only to allies. No great attention was paid by the West to the importance of Swedish neutrality to continued Finnish independence. Only in 1950 did the campaign subside and were the fears of a military vacuum in the North laid to rest by strong Swedish defense efforts.

Sweden's persistent neutrality should have made a clear impression in Moscow, since American and British pressure was hardly a secret. Still, the suspicious Russians probably looked upon Stockholm's motives with even more cold skepticism than the Americans: Here was a capitalist country with strong cultural, economic, and emotional ties to the West, an historic aversion to Russia, and a democratic distaste for Russia's dictatorial system, a military machine among the strongest in Europe managed by conservative officials who saw the East as the only threat. Clearly, this neutral country had a problem of credibility.

But negative opinion in both the East and the West encouraged rather than dissuaded the Swedes in their efforts to develop a neutral option for Scandinavia. If a defense grouping was allied to the West, it would clearly provoke the Soviet Union and jeopardize Finland, a matter which was of concern not only for Sweden but for the other Scandinavians as well, particularly Norway, which shared an 800-kilometer border with Finland. A neutral Scandinavian bloc implied sacrifices for Stockholm because it meant that Sweden would have to be the main guarantor of its military strength. In return, however, the security of the country would benefit through the decreased risk of a separate attack limited to Sweden and a greater chance that the Scandinavian area would stay outside a war between East and West.

Denmark, which wished to remain outside the great power blocs then being created, supported Sweden. Norway, which was more inclined than the other two countries to seek protection under an Anglo-American umbrella, insisted that a link be established to the Western powers believing that only in that case would they be willing to supply modern military equipment to a Scandinavian union. The Norwegians, from their bitter experience in World War II, had little hope of escaping involvement in a third world war, especially if they stood alone with no powerful protector. The differences among the Scandinavians could not be bridged and the project was aborted. Norway and Denmark joined NATO in April 1949.

The Soviet position all through the early postwar years was consistently negative toward a "Scandinavian bloc." *Izvestija* in December 1948 summed up the various proposals of this kind as being all inspired by Washington: A Swedish-Norwegian-Finnish common defense scheme in March 1940 directed against the Soviet Union; the idea in 1945 a Nordic union politically guided by Great Britain; the Marshall plan, which foresaw an economic Scandinavian union which would lead to a military bloc linked to the West; the Swedish initiative, which if realized would necessarily gravitate toward the West, as could clearly be seen from the Norwegian posture ("U.S.A. would play the role of the rider and the Scandinavian countries that of the horse," as a newspaper colleague in Leningrad had already put it). That position had been taken as soon as the first rumors started in early 1947 about Scandinavian defense talks.

As the issue became whether a neutral Scandinavian defense union should be created or whether Norway and Denmark should join NATO, one might have expected that Moscow would prefer the lesser evil and soften its criticism of the neutral Scandinavian option. In early 1949, that seemed to be the expectation in official Swedish and Norwegian circles. Public

Soviet sources, however, indicate that this was an incorrect assumption. Such a grouping, it was believed, would in any case gravitate to the West, drawing Sweden also in that direction. The Soviets had no confidence in Sweden's will and capacity to maintain its neutrality and lead its smaller brother countries along this path. Suspicions in Moscow were also fueled by the lively debate going on in Sweden, where influential media and a part of the opposition advocated close defense links with the West. While Sweden's own neutrality at this time received occasional grudging support, mixed with much criticism, from Moscow, the idea that a Scandinavian bloc would pursue a similar policy was thus not credible.

Added to this lack of confidence in the ability of small countries to resist great capitalist powers was a tactical "ideological" consideration. The "two camps" concept still dominated Soviet propaganda, serving the purpose of cementing the bloc in Eastern Europe and encouraging Communist parties in the West. Neutrality had no place in this strategy. The firm belief in the Kremlin was that the Scandinavians as a group would be tied to the West both economically and politically.

A few years later, in 1952, there were some indications that Moscow might have had second thoughts on the subject of a neutral Scandinavian defense union. A Soviet campaign to get Denmark and Norway out of NATO hinted at such a possibility. But in the shadow of the Korean War, the Scandinavians had lost interest in that option. Finland's Prime Minister Kekkonen recommended neutrality for Norway and Denmark at this time, but received only a polite but chilly rebuke from these countries.

Moscow had not officially intervened in the early Scandinavian discussions about a defense union or an association with the West, but had expressed its opinion through public media. Rumor also had it that Soviet troops were massed on the Finnish-Soviet border, perhaps as a pressure tactic on the Scandinavians. In early 1949, when the issue came to a head, Moscow went into formal action. On 29 January 1949, a white paper was published on the Atlantic pact, in which Western efforts to draw the Scandinavian states into that collaboration were detailed. On the same day, Molotov talked in *Pravda* about the "strange behavior of the Norwegian government" in trying to bypass opposition to these schemes for an Atlantic Alliance by proceeding with a Scandinavian pact which was designed to lead these states into the North Atlantic sphere.

The Soviet ambassador in Oslo delivered a note in which the Atlantic pact was described as "a group of states with aggressive aims, whose initiators intend to procure military airfields and naval bases in various parts of the globe, particularly in areas belonging to states close to Soviet borders." The Norwegian government was asked to clarify its attitude toward the Atlantic pact and also whether it would undertake any obligations as to military air or naval bases on Norwegian territory.   It was clear that Moscow's concern centered on overseas bases for the American Strategic Air Command. Indeed, the major threat to the U.S.S.R. would be represented in the years to come by U.S. and British bomber forces operating from a large network of bases around the periphery of the Soviet Union.

Oslo's answer indicated that it intended to join the Alliance, but it also stated that Norway would never permit the use of its territory for aggressive purposes nor would it "adhere to any treaty which contains obligations to open bases for the armed forces of other nations as long as Norway is not under attack or subjected to a threat of an attack."

Moscow was not satisfied with these Norwegian protestations of pacific intentions. The Soviet ambassador returned with a new note in which it was pointed out that Oslo could use any "provocative rumors or cooked-up lies about a threat of an attack on Norway" to allow foreign powers to establish war bases or move armed forces into Norwegian territory.   Moscow proposed a nonaggression treaty between the two countries "if there were any doubts about the good-neighborly intentions of the U.S.S.R. with respect to Norway." Oslo's negative answer, referring to the undertaking of the signatories to the U.N. Charter not to attack each other, was communicated after its decision to adhere to the Atlantic pact had already been made. In the meantime, however, there was considerable nervousness in Norway, indicative of these troubled times, that the Russians would take hostile, even armed, action, suddenly occupying Finnmark or Svalbard, for instance. Indeed, the Soviets reacted bitterly to the Atlantic pact decisions by the Scandinavians, but no evidence exists of any aggressive plans.

Both Norway and Denmark were aware of Soviet sensibilities when they joined the Atlantic Alliance. The restrictions Norway placed on the location of NATO bases on its territory (and later other restrictions as to atomic weapons) were explained by its foreign minister. There was a risk "that the Soviet government might invoke the Soviet-Finnish treaty and demand military bases on Finnish territory, apart from the Porkkala base, directed against northern Norwegian or northern Swedish territory. . . . Apart from such Nordic considerations the Norwegian government paid much attention to its general relations with the U.S.S.R. . . . having become better acquainted during the Svalbard negotiations in 1945 with the security policy considerations of the Soviet Union as to its northwestern regions and the adjoining Arctic areas." Another consideration was the resentment that would be caused by the presence of foreign military personnel in recently occupied Norway, which was highly jealous of its independence.

The restraints in Norwegian NATO policies were partly due to internal considerations, since a large segment of the ruling Social Democratic party was skeptical of NATO membership as such and had to be reassured by this moderate solution. However, from the outset the restrictions were explained mainly by the need not to provoke the U.S.S.R., both because that would compromise Norwegian security and because it might have negative consequences for other Nordic countries. The Norwegian restrictions did not create any problems within the Alliance: No great need existed for additional air bases; Norwegian airfields could, in any case, be made available in a war situation; the Americans and the British were unwilling to provoke the Soviet Union for no good reason. Thus, the Norwegian policy had support from the Alliance.

Given the overriding Norwegian concern not to provoke the U.S.S.R., there is some logic in the consistent Soviet refusal to accept this policy as a unilateral defense restriction to be interpreted by Norway alone. On the contrary, Moscow, regarding the base policy as a binding obligation, took it upon itself to interpret it in a restrictive manner.

Denmark, at this time, played a less prominent role in Soviet thinking, as indicated by media and official activity. Moscow did send a memorandum to Copenhagen warning it about the danger of participation in NATO, to which the Danes replied only that "Denmark will not join a policy pursuing aggressive goals." In Danish parliamentary debates, government spokesmen denied that foreign bases would be established in Denmark and confirmed its interest not to provoke the Russians. Denmark was paid little attention by Moscow partly because it was, correctly, seen as positioned in the middle and dependent for its decisions upon Norway and Sweden. The Soviets saw it as a foregone conclusion that Denmark would adhere to the Atlantic pact when Norway had made up its mind.

"Isolated neutrality" would indeed have been an almost impossible option for Denmark, given its geographic position and historical experience. From Washington came the message that Denmark would not be protected unless it were a full member of the Western Alliance, because Danish territory in and of itself was not sufficiently important to Western defense interests. Soviet exits from the Baltic could perhaps be better prevented by armed action from southern Norway than by closing the straits. Denmark's adherance to the Atlantic pact was important mainly because it solved the problem of Greenland. Danish diplomats thought that Russia, on the other hand, had much to gain from positions in Denmark, flanking Sweden and providing better outlets for the Soviet submarine fleet. If Denmark remained neutral, it would be a good prize which could be grabbed at low risk to the Russian bear. The Nordic option, which was much preferred by the politicians, had now evaporated.

Whatever Moscow thought of these strategic considerations, it did not get overly excited when Copenhagen in March 1949 joined the Atlantic Alliance, a decision which generated only routine criticism. The Norwegian entry could have posed problems for Finland, had there not been sensitivity in Moscow to Swedish reaction to a possible Soviet move in Finland's direction. Denmark's stand, however, with its similar but less clearly specified base restrictions, was not at the time regarded as likely to provoke the Russians to take any action except perhaps the positioning of Soviet troops closer to Danish borders in occupied zones in Germany. In fact, the Russians did nothing except publish condemnatory articles.

Soviet behavior in the 1940s and early 1950s served to divide Scandinavia. Norway and Denmark were linked to NATO with certain military restraints; Sweden remained neutral. The main points in the Soviet position were opposition to the Scandinavian defense community and acquiescence, although highly unwilling, in Danish and Norwegian NATO membership. Half-hearted Soviet attempts thereafter to encourage the Danes and the Norwegians to leave NATO were combined with a very firm and sometimes threatening attitude toward the important issues of nuclear weapons and American or German base rights in these countries. The outcome on these matters was reasonably satisfactory to Moscow.

*Iceland, Greenland, the Faroe Islands,
and Jan Mayen*

It is appropriate at this point to touch on the role of Iceland, Greenland, and the small territories in the North Atlantic, the Faroe Islands belonging to Denmark and Jan Mayen, a Norwegian possession. From the Soviet perspective, they were principally military and strategic strongpoints exploited by the other superpower; therefore, Soviet policies must be directed in peacetime toward encouraging political dissatisfaction with such use, and in crises or wartime toward minimizing their military significance. The strategic picture in the North Atlantic is dealt with later in this book. What follows is a brief background to Soviet policies.

Iceland acquired statehood in December 1918, but a union was immediately created with the former colonial power, Denmark, which retained control of defense and foreign policy. German occupation of Denmark in April 1940 allowed Iceland to assume its own sovereignty. Soon afterward, British troops occupied Iceland to prevent German control over the country. One year later, the United States took over from the British and promised to recognize Icelandic independence and sovereignty. Finally, on 16 June 1944, the Althing, the Icelandic parliament, created the Republic of Iceland.

The American troops should have left Iceland at the end of World War II, according to the 1941 agreement. Instead, Washington requested that three American bases be set up in the country. The Icelanders refused and the Althing soon demanded the immediate withdrawal of U.S. troops, which took place in 1947. Concurrently, however, the Americans were given permission to use Keflavik airport for five years. Later, Iceland joined in the Marshall plan (two-thirds of its trade was with the West) and became a charter member of NATO without ever participating in its military organization, since the country does not maintain its own armed forces.

When Iceland joined the Atlantic Alliance, it had been told that the West had no need to set up bases or to station troops there, despite the fact that the country did not have an army of its own. The Korean War and East-West tension in the early 1950s soon changed this Western attitude. An agreement in 1951 permitted the stationing of U.S. forces, later limited to 3,000 men, on the Keflavik naval airbase and at various radar and communication stations. Over the years, various demands have been made in internal Icelandic political debate, particularly by the Communist party, to have the Americans leave, but the international situation has prevented any change. Washington has all along placed great value on the bases on both Iceland and Greenland, which was evidenced as early as 1947-48 during the discussions preceding the Atlantic pact.

The Russians have taken an active interest in relations with Iceland since the early postwar years. A trade agreement was concluded in 1946, when Moscow showed a readiness to spend considerably to establish itself as a major market for Iceland's key export commodity, fish. This political gesture did not bring any concrete results. Trade, advantageous to both parties, has since fluctuated but has never greatly influenced the political situation.

The 1951 agreement was described by the Russians as "making Iceland virtually a military base of the U.S.A." Detente in the mid-1950s seemed to work to Soviet advantage. The Icelandic parliament demanded a revision of the agreement with the United States and a withdrawal of American troops. When Communists entered the government in 1956, that position, which depended on continued better East-West relations, became even more pronounced. The Soviet invasion of Hungary ended all that and a new troop agreement was concluded at the end of that year.

The Russians, however, did not give up. In December 1957, a note was delivered in Reykjavik guaranteeing Soviet respect for Iceland's neutrality in case the Americans were told to close their bases. The Communist fishing minister received considerable credits in Moscow toward the purchase of fishing vessels. The Soviet Union also promised to recognize the extension of the Icelandic fishing limit to twelve miles, a proposal which had been met with strong opposition by the NATO partners, principally the U.K. The goal, however-- Iceland's security choice--still eluded these Soviet overtures.

In 1958, Soviet President Bulganin sent letters to the Scandinavian NATO members (see below), including Iceland, warning them not to permit the stationing of nuclear weapons on their territory. Reykjavik replied that only defensive weapons existed and would exist on Icelandic territory. The question of installing nuclear weapons in the country had never come up for consideration. Iceland has since stated that it must give its approval to any American deployment of nuclear weapons in the country. This position has been accepted by

Washington, even though the Americans maintain as a principle never to deny or confirm the presence of nuclear weapons on U.S. bases, including Keflavik. It is quite clear furthermore that no request to deploy such weapons has been made so far and that such a request would be refused in peacetime. Iceland's official non-committal position is that the matter would be examined upon such a request "in crisis situations." Russian propaganda, directed essentially to radical groups in the country, has raised the question whether the Americans are not after all hiding nuclear weapons on Iceland or at least preparing to use the country as a center for its nuclear-weapon strategy in wartime. In direct dealings with the Icelandic government, however, the Russians have been more polite. Thus Kosygin, welcoming the Icelandic prime minister to Moscow in 1977, expressed special satisfaction over the absence of nuclear weapons in Iceland.

Nuclear weapons are subject to heated internal debate in Iceland as in other Nordic countries. Recent Althing resolutions confirm government policy not to permit nuclear weapons on Iceland in peacetime but to keep open the possibility to allow such weapons to be stationed there in war or crisis situations. All parties are in favor of a Nordic nuclear-free zone, but the government has chosen to define such a zone as covering a large region including the Baltic, the eastern North Atlantic, and the Barents Sea, a proposition which has but a minimal chance of gaining support from the superpowers.

NATO is in the process of modernizing its forces and equipment on Iceland in response to increased Soviet air and naval presence in the region. Orion and AWACS early warning systems are being complemented by two additional radar stations for air surveillance to be placed in the northeastern and northwestern parts of Iceland. Soviet attention has long since concentrated on the strategic services offered by Iceland to the U.S., centered principally around the Keflavik airbase. The main points in the Soviet "list of accusations" are that the Keflavik airbase has become "an unsinkable giant aircraft carrier" with a large air wing composed of attack aircraft, anti-submarine aircraft, and AWACS systems; that radio navigation stations have been built on other parts of Iceland to guide nuclear-weapon submarines; and that the Sound Surveillance System (SOSUS) exists to detect Soviet submarines in the GIUK gap between Greenland, Iceland, and the United Kingdom.

Moscow and Washington both regard Iceland as an important asset in NATO's strategic position in the North Atlantic, which has grown increasingly essential for both powers. Russian criticism has been sharp, but it has been mitigated somewhat by the knowledge that NATO's alternative to Iceland as a base area would presumably be northern Norway. If that came about, it would be even more of a nuisance and a danger for the Soviet Union.

Greenland was the subject of an agreement between the Allied powers and Denmark in 1941 and served during the war as an important base area between the U.S. and the U.K. Moscow stressed the strategic importance of Greenland in the early postwar years and criticized American ambitions there. Molotov found occasion in 1947 to point out that the Americans totally disregarded Danish sovereignty over this territory. No doubt the Russians were uneasy about such an American strongpoint giving the U.S. the capability "to make one jump into Eurasia." In 1951, American base rights were confirmed. Early warning stations were set up during the 1950s to detect bombers and were later complemented with systems to warn against intercontinental ballistic missiles, as the polar regions were brought into the realm of strategic interest.

Since the introduction of home rule in 1979, the left-wing Siumut party has been in power in Greenland. However, according to Bjol, there has been no anti-base movement in Greenland comparable to the one in Iceland. On the contrary, the local government has on several occasions reiterated Greenland's adherence to NATO as part of the Danish realm. For one thing, the main American base of Thule is much farther from populated areas than Keflavik is from Reykjavik. Moreover, the Greenlanders have been quite aware of the economic advantages of the American presence to their country.

On the other hand, when they decided to leave the EEC, economic considerations were hardly decisive. Although the mother country, Denmark, has retained control over Greenland's security policy, it might prove difficult to go against strong local opposition should it develop.

The Faroe Islands and Jan Mayen have never played a major military role in the eastern North Atlantic, although the NATO installations there form part of the Alliance's net of early warning stations in this area, staffed principally by non-American personnel.

THE EARLY 1950s: INTERNATIONAL TENSION AND SCANDINAVIA

The early 1950s was a period of constant high international tension manifested in the outbreak of the Korean War. Moscow clearly believed that the Western Alliance posed a definite threat to the Soviet Union and its allies. While NATO's conventional forces in Europe were far too small to represent any danger, the menace of the atom bomb could not be disregarded as the Americans acquired airbases stretching from the Atlantic to the Persian Gulf. Internal rebellions in Eastern Europe of the kind that were later to take place in Berlin in 1953 and Hungary in 1956 might in 1950 have posed a much graver problem for the Soviet Union if the Americans had tried to dissuade Moscow from intervening by nuclear threats. Clearly, the U.S. meant to push back the Soviet sphere of influence. Internal cohesion in the "socialist camp" was easier to maintain if the outside threat was painted in stark colors. There seemed to be no room for neutral shades.

The West had had no great fears of a massive Russian attack in Europe until the Korean War, when the Soviets seemed to demonstrate their aggressiveness and their willingness to take risks. The Alliance alone, linking U.S. military strength to Europe's defense, then no longer appeared to provide enough security. Military muscle must be added; the potential aggressor would have to be met on the border between East and West. This frontline defense required that West Germany be rearmed.

West German rearmament was a major threat to postwar Soviet positions and the prevention of such a development became a principal aim of Soviet foreign policy. A German army might provide the political-military impetus for provoking and exploiting, under the American nuclear umbrella, a revolt in the East European satellites. The Berlin blockade had failed to dissuade the West from establishing a unified West German state. Fortunately, from the Soviet perspective, France prevented until 1954-55 the inclusion of Germany in NATO and the buildup of a modern German armed force. For a time, Moscow felt less threatened in Europe.

It is likely that this situation proved beneficial for Soviet-Finnish relations, which had been smooth and amical since 1950 when the Social Democratic minority government, opposed by local Communists and Moscow media, had been succeeded by a more broadly based government under Kekkonen. When West Germany finally did join NATO in 1954-55 and efforts began to build a modern West German army, the Soviets made no threats toward Finland. Helsinki was asked, however, on different occasions in 1954 to subscribe to Soviet views on European security problems and to support Moscow's proposal for an all-European collective security system, but it managed to achieve fairly anodyne wordings in joint communiques. The Russians, it seemed, did not want to rock the Nordic boat, which now steered a reasonably satisfactory course. Gradually, more confidence crept into Soviet-Finnish relations, and Finland's decision to keep out of great-power conflicts, as stated in the FCMA treaty, was respected. Thus no efforts were made to enroll Finland in the Warsaw Pact, which was created in 1955.

In 1951, Norway and Denmark, supported by the United States, embarked upon a considerable strengthening of their armed forces and a closer coordination of their defense planning with the Western Alliance.

The Scandinavian members of NATO accepted the American proposal for a military structure within the Alliance, with common armed forces under unitary command, and pledged a portion of their own forces for use in wartime by the Alliance. NATO's "Northern region" was placed under the authority of the Supreme Allied Command Atlantic (SACLANT) and was delineated to embrace Denmark, Norway, and Schleswig-Holstein, plus the Baltic. Soviet policy in the North came to be directed primarily against these measures.

Moscow sent a note to the Norwegian government (15 October 1951) roundly criticizing it for "permitting Norwegian territory to be used by the armed forces of the aggressive Altantic pact . . . and putting Norwegian forces under the American military command which directs and plans military preparations in Norway." The Russians complained that NATO had been allowed to set up headquarters for its Northern Command outside Oslo; that Norway had made preparations to receive foreign troops on its territory and was expanding naval and air bases, some of them close to Soviet territory; and that American and British air and navy units were conducting exercises in Norway.

The Soviet government particularly complained that Spitzbergen and Bear Island had been put under the authority of the Supreme Commander of NATO naval forces, permitting the American command to conduct military maneuvers in the area around these islands in direct violation of the 1920 Svalbard treaty. Norway's actions damaged Soviet economic and security interests and went against its earlier promises and international agreements.

The Norwegian response refuted the accusation of aggressive intentions on its own part or on the part of NATO and referred to Norway's definition of its base policy, which did indeed permit most of what the Russians objected to, such as preparations to receive foreign troops, Allied exercises in Norway, etc. Oslo maintained that the Svalbard treaty was being scrupulously adhered to, since no military fortifications or bases were being set up within the island group. These explanations did not satisfy Moscow, which in its reply insisted that NATO was preparing for a new war, as demonstrated by the ring of bases established around the U.S.S.R. and the arms race. Norway had joined this aggressive bloc even though it had been offered a nonaggression treaty by the Soviet Union.

As for Denmark, Soviet criticism concentrated on the impending military exercises in the Baltic (Operation Main Brace) and the "breach of a Danish promise" not to let foreign armed forces enter Bornholm. The main point, however, as expressed in a Soviet government declaration in October 1952, concerned Denmark's purported intention to "permit foreign armed forces to stay in Danish territory in peacetime . . . and thus to turn Denmark into a base for foreign troops." The Danish government was reminded that it had promised not to pursue a policy of aggression against the Soviet Union: "To give military bases to foreign armed forces will be regarded as an act that creates a threat to the U.S.S.R. and other countries in the Baltic area. The Soviet government puts all responsibility for the possible effects of such a policy on the Danish government."

The Danish government had in fact made a decision "to consider a NATO offer of stationing in peacetime foreign air forces in Denmark," and had expressed itself in a positive manner while claiming that this did not imply any "base rights." The NATO offer concerned 150 to 200 aircraft with crews and ground personnel.

The Danish response to the Soviet declaration denied any aggressive intent but did not comment on the purported plans. The Norwegian foreign minister went on record as welcoming such a strengthening of the defenses of Denmark and, indirectly, Norway, pointing out that Norway could not take similar action on its own given its declaration in 1949 not to station foreign forces in Norway. The Russians returned to the attack in January 1953 with a detailed *aide-memoire* containing essentially the same accusations, now couched in more violent language "as the reply of the Danish government cannot be considered satisfactory." Special emphasis was given to Bornholm and to German participation in the collective aggressive efforts of the Western bloc, which obviously was preparing for a new world war. Denmark's action ran counter to protestations that it would not participate in plans of aggression against the Soviet Union and the People's Democracies. To establish foreign military bases on Danish territory in peacetime could not be in Denmark's own interest "as it would create a threat to its security and independence."

The main Soviet message was that "By entering the North Atlantic bloc Denmark became a part of an aggressive military group . . . preparing a world war. By accepting foreign troops in peacetime Denmark becomes a direct participant in the war now under preparation." The Polish government chimed in with a declaration that Bornholm was being prepared to become "the point of departure for the war preparations of the new Nazi Wehrmacht."

The Soviet declaration never received a Danish answer. The Soviets did reap some practical results from this massive onslaught, however. The Danish foreign minister, while refuting the Soviet interpretation of Danish promises regarding Bornholm, stated that, whatever had been said in 1946, the Danish government had de facto followed a policy of not permitting foreign troops to be stationed on that island. It also intended to continue that policy. Somewhat later, a final decision was made by the new Social Democratic government not to accept the NATO offer to station air units in Denmark. The decision did not apply to Greenland, where American forces had been stationed since 1951. The conclusion in Moscow must have been that Copenhagen was susceptible to pressure but also that the Danes recognized reasonable limits to its military policies.

Stockholm had its share of bilateral troubles during these tense years. Moscow carefully and suspiciously monitored Sweden's military policies and its rapidly expanding arms investments. Swedish naval maneuvers, which coincided with Operation Main Brace, caused Soviet allegations of Swedish collaboration with NATO. Various spy operations were uncovered by the Swedes and envenomed the atmosphere. Swedish Communists faithfully echoed Moscow's media attacks but had but little impact on domestic opinion. From a strong showing in immediate postwar elections (11.2 percent in 1946) they had rapidly dwindled to between 4 percent and 5 percent in the early 1950s.

In April 1951, *Bolshevik*, the Soviet Communist party's theoretical mouthpiece, published a major article entitled "Sweden's rightist Social Democrats--the lackeys of American imperialism," possibly the most virulent authoritative attack that has ever been written against official Sweden. The title gave an adequate description of the tenor and content of the article, which painted in stark colors the sins of Swedish governments since prewar times. The most recent crimes included aid to American aggression in Korea, support of the Acheson plan in the U.N. aimed at subserving that organization to U.S. policies, participation in U.S. trade embargoes against the Soviet bloc, etc. There was some truth to the *Bolshevik* accusations regarding trade restrictions imposed by Swedish industrial enterprises and anti-Soviet feelings in Sweden, but the article grotesquely distorted Swedish government positions and did not seem to perturb official Stockholm. Stalinist media rhetoric had lost its impact through constant hyperbole and was not followed up in official contacts.

Neutrality was a difficult policy to pursue during these years. Pressures were mounting from both sides. Obviously, for a small capitalist country like Sweden, anchored culturally and commercially in the Western world, persuasion from that side was more difficult to withstand. A special problem was created by the American-sponsored embargo policy against Eastern Europe in the late 1940s and early 1950s. The neutral Swedes were informally pressed to apply certain restrictions to the export and trans-shipment of goods included in the COCOM lists. The Americans went further and, without great success, tried to push the Swedish government to limit exports of iron ore, special steel, and ball bearings. Some individual Swedish firms, such as SKF, followed COCOM guidelines and claimed to Eastern European customers that their production capacity was fully booked. The Russians expressed indignation over U.S. economic pressures on Sweden (*Tass*, March 1949), but did not try to exert any real pressure of their own. Soviet and Eastern European clout was in any case minimal, since their market-share for most Swedish firms was only a few percentage points.

Another bone of contention was the more active Swedish pursuit of "the Wallenberg case," the mystery surrounding the disappearance of a Swedish diplomat--the savior of thousands of Hungarian Jews--who was imprisoned in 1945 by Russian troops occupying Budapest. That question came to envenom Soviet-Swedish relations all through the postwar years as Moscow was unable or unwilling to satisfy Swedish demands for full disclosure of what had happened to the Swedish diplomat after his capture. In 1957, Soviet authorities for the first time officially admitted that Wallenberg had died in captivity and blamed Stalin's security officials. Over the years, however, a series of witnesses have testified that Wallenberg was alive after 1947, the date of death given by Moscow, prompting new Swedish demands for full clarification.

In mid-June 1952, two Swedish reconnaissance planes were shot down by Soviet aircraft in the Baltic (the "Catalina affair"). The Swedish version of the episode was that an unarmed military plane with a crew of eight had disappeared on 13 June over what was clearly international waters. During rescue operations three days later another aircraft was shot down by MIG-15s, also over international waters. The Soviet version was that on these dates Soviet aircraft had spotted foreign planes in Soviet airspace and had performed their duty, which was "to force such aircraft to land on a local airfield, or if they resist, to open fire." The Soviets claimed that on 16 June, the foreign aircraft, which had been identified as Swedish, had first opened fire which was returned; on 13 June, bad weather had prevented identification and the aircraft was chased away.

The Soviet government refused to refer the matter to an international body such as the International Court, as proposed by the Swedes, maintaining that "to defend the borders of the U.S.S.R. is the duty and obligation of the Soviet state." The Soviet statements, while refuting entirely the Swedish allegations and repeating Moscow's version, were fairly moderate in tone and did not contain innuendos of Swedish collaboration with the West--a charge that was made by local Communists in Sweden-- or threats of any Soviet reaction. Moscow probably did not wish to inflame the already highly emotional debate in Sweden or to provide ammunition to those in Sweden who advocated defense links with the West. It also explicitly refrained from questioning the right of Swedish military aircraft to conduct whatever operations they wished over international waters. Its action did carry a harsh military-political message, however. If the planes had crossed into Soviet airspace, as the Russians alleged, it was most certainly desirable to teach the intruders a lesson, particularly as this was not the first such incident. If, as the Swedes claimed and were willing to prove, the planes had not crossed Soviet borders, the Russians had given a warning that military reconnaissance flights too close to Soviet borders would be in some danger. "Provocative" behavior might be costly for a small neutral state, not least because the Russians could not be expected to distinguish Swedish planes from NATO ones.

While the incident had a fairly positive aftermath in that Sweden and the U.S.S.R. concluded an agreement in 1954 on the rescue of crews from endangered ships or aircraft, Soviet suspicions of Swedish policies were mirrored in articles such as the one which appeared in *Novoje Vremja* in the spring of 1954:

> As the American war planners give Sweden increasing attention, the Swedish government continues its protestations of neutrality without however reacting in any way against the provocative speeches of Swedish military leaders. The generals Nordenskjold, Svedlund, and Jung not only insist on a further expansion of the arms race but also demand a general association of the Swedish defense structure with the West. They maintain that in case of war the Americans should be given military strong-points [in Sweden]. Those who govern Sweden have tied their country to the Marshall plan, which ruins the country, and without parliamentary approval they have decided that Sweden should join the

Council of Europe. In view of these facts the
Swedish assertions of neutrality and promises not
to participate in any aggressive policy have
become empty maneuvering.

NEW DEPARTURES IN SOVIET FOREIGN POLICY:
THE THAW OF 1955

Autumn 1955 saw a series of Soviet detente efforts with
importance for the Nordic countries. The Soviet Union handed
back to Finland the base area of Porkkala and extended the
FCMA treaty by twenty years. The center of the Soviet military
presence had shifted from the Gulf of Finland to the Murmansk
coast and the southern Baltic, leaving Finland less exposed. The
headquarters of the Baltic Fleet was moved from Kronstadt to
Kaliningrad, easing the return of the Porkkala naval base.
Finland was thus able to establish "neutrality," and Finnish
sovereignty was further manifested in its membership in the
United Nations. Moscow dropped its earlier objections to
Finnish membership in the Nordic Council, which Helsinki soon
joined, excluding however participation in any security or
military discussions. Finland also decided to participate in the
regular yearly meetings of the Nordic foreign ministers. Finnish
neutrality was officially recognized by Moscow in 1956, when
Khrushchev explicitly named this country among the European
neutrals. The margins of Finnish independence seemed to
broaden.

Finland had lost most of its military-strategic interest for
the Soviet Union, as Khrushchev himself stated in 1957, but the
international political context was also a decisive factor.
Moscow's detente policies had been in full swing since early
1955: Austria was given independence coupled to a permanently
neutral status; Tito's national communism was ostentatiously
accepted in a visit to Belgrade by the top Soviet leaders; the
nonaligned countries in the Third World were assiduously
courted; and Moscow made concrete disarmament proposals to
the Western powers.

"Neutrality" acquired increased value as Soviet leaders gradually abandoned Stalin's perception of international politics as two camps constantly warring against each other, peace and socialism against capitalism and imperialism, where no third force was possible.

The concept also became a useful symbol to be exploited in the Third World. The new countries wanted to be nonaligned between East and West; therefore, the U.S.S.R. must change its negative attitude toward neutrality and try to describe this policy as being more in line with its own stand on world affairs. The European neutrals--Austria, Finland, Switzerland, and Sweden--were thus praised for their policies and admonished to adopt an even more "positive neutrality." Amical relations with these countries demonstrated to the Third World the good intentions of the U.S.S.R.

The gestures toward Finland laid the groundwork for a diplomatic offensive to improve relations with the Scandinavian countries. The style was new--less pressure and more wooing to promote Scandinavian policies that accommodated basic Soviet interests. The prime ministers of Denmark, Norway, and Sweden were invited to Moscow. Cultural and commercial contacts were expanded. A Swedish naval contingent visited Leningrad, the first foreign warships to visit that city since the war.

During this period, Sweden's neutrality was unequivocally recognized and assumed to be permanent. In the joint communique after the visit of the Swedish prime minister to Moscow in early 1956, the Soviet side "declared that the Soviet Union, as before, will respect this nonaligned and peaceful policy of Sweden." In what became a Russian habit, Moscow insisted that a neutral policy must be "active" and contribute through political initiatives to the peaceful solution of international problems. The Swedes replied that a small neutral country normally has no reason to meddle in great-power disputes. Moscow continued to view Sweden's military, particularly its generals, with suspicion and rated them as far too strong to serve only the needs of this small, neutral country.

At approximately this time, both Molotov and Gromyko made public proposals to Norway and Denmark to follow Swedish neutral policies and, additionally, to conclude security guarantee treaties with the Soviet Union. This theme, a neutral Northern Europe, including Iceland, became prominent in Soviet propaganda during the next few years.

This approach yielded no concrete results, but rather confirmed the status quo. The Norwegians clearly stated that they would not "give foreign forces any strongholds on Norwegian territory as long as Norway was not under attack or the threat thereof." Similar Danish declarations made it clear that no Scandinavian NATO member would jeopardize relations in the North by any concessions to military planners in NATO which were not clearly in their own interest.

The general pattern of Scandinavian-Soviet relations had thus been established. Norway and Denmark tried to combine NATO membership with the kind of military restraint that would satisfy reasonable Soviet security demands as they defined them. In some cases, that policy seemed to be influenced somewhat by Soviet pressure or threats (Danish positions on the stationing of NATO air personnel and the tactical nuclear weapons issue, for example). Another explanation for these policies might be that the governments of these countries had become more aware of the foreign policy implications of certain decisions. In other cases, however, Soviet blandishments or "charm offensives" created a more relaxed atmosphere but did not yield any tangible benefits to Moscow. Aggressive Soviet behavior, such as violation of territory or violent action (as in the Catalina affair), never paid off but only gave ammunition to those who favored stronger pro-NATO stands.

While Swedish links to the West were viewed with suspicion, the Russians increasingly favored the neutrality policy in principle. Media attacks, if not motivated by the lingering two-camps ideology, were presumably often intended more to keep Swedish politicians on their guard against less prudent opposition members or military men than to describe real feelings in the Kremlin on Swedish neutrality. As has often been the case in Soviet propaganda, accusations were preemptive, intended to evoke denials which would prevent future unpleasant developments.

BACK TO THE COLD WAR?

With the Porkkala base returned to the Finns, Russian troops no longer traveling on Finnish railways, and Scandinavian prime ministers paying friendly visits to Moscow, the Nordic scene seemed particularly relaxed. This phase was short-lived, however. Hungary put a stop to detente. The Scandinavian governments postponed a Khrushchev-Bulganin visit to their countries. Spies were discovered working for the KGB. The German issue resurfaced and a temporary chill entered Scandinavian-Soviet relations as the nuclear issue also became prominent. Finally, Khrushchev himself canceled his planned visit to the three Scandinavian capitals in 1959, referring to anti-Soviet campaigns there. Perhaps he had abandoned earlier hopes of launching a nuclear-free zone in the North, or maybe he had simply found a good and timely excuse to put off a visit which had become awkward since the upcoming important journey to the United States had to be prepared for.

The Soviet inclination to view the Baltic as a *mare clausum* took more concrete form in the mid-1950s. *Izvestija* stated the Soviet position (6 September 1957): "The Baltic can and will finally become a sea of peace and benefit to all people living along its coasts. Four-fifths of the coastline lies in the zone of states that in one way or another are active for peaceful coexistence. Countries that belong to NATO, Denmark and FRG, take up only a small part of the Baltic coast. Certainly if one or the other Baltic state decided to quit NATO it would simplify the efforts to turn that area into a sea of peace."

In 1959, East Germany put forward a draft nonaggression treaty among the Baltic states, no doubt with Soviet benediction. Khrushchev proposed in 1959 an agreement "on a zone free from rockets and nuclear weapons on the Scandinavian peninsula and in the Baltic area," an idea that was rejected by Sweden, which argued that Soviet installations in the area would not be covered. Khrushchev, in a speech in Szczecin on 17 July, replied indirectly that he had not eliminated the possibility that Soviet territory might be included in the nuclear-free area, but the issue was not pursued. Nor was the Scandinavian reception of that idea encouraging. The "Sea of Peace" concept had already been criticized by the Swedes, who referred to the importance of keeping the Baltic free for all traffic (Unden, 26 June 1959).

The Soviet proposal for a peaceful Baltic did not entail a willingness to limit its own conventional military forces in the area. Indeed, a massive Soviet buildup of air and sea power was actually undertaken. The corresponding Western efforts, including the construction of a German navy, the increased German role in NATO after 1954-55, and the linkage to Danish defense, created a sharp conflict in Soviet-Danish relations.

NATO elaborated plans for a Baltic naval command, under the authority of the "Northern region," with the participation particularly of the two Baltic nations, West Germany and Denmark. These plans quickly evoked highly critical comments in the Soviet press. A message from Bulganin to the Danish prime minister, H. C. Hansen, on 12 December 1957 referred to the NATO plans as "measures which complicate the situation in the Baltic area and concern the security interest of other Baltic states." Implementation of the plan was delayed several years and finally was merged into a general reorganization of the defense of the Baltic region. On 31 August 1961, at a time when East-West tension was at its peak (the Berlin wall was erected on 13 August and the U.S.S.R. had recently resumed atmospheric nuclear tests), plans were published for a unitary NATO wartime command for this area, composed of army, navy, and air force units in Denmark, Schleswig-Holstein, and the Baltic. These units would consist mainly of West German and Danish forces with a Danish general in command. A German admiral would be appointed to head the naval forces.

The Soviet reaction was swift and firm. The Soviet government declared that these plans were clear evidence that "given the relation of strength, the Danish armed forces will in practice be entirely subordinated to the West German military command." Denmark would thus "be drawn into the adventures of West German generals contrary to Denmark's own interest and potentially with serious consequences for Denmark." Since these West German militarists wanted revision of German borders, atomic weapons in the Bundeswehr, and new and better bases in foreign countries, but were opposed to a peace treaty between the two German states and a normalization of the status of West Berlin, Denmark had chosen a dangerous road. The creation of the unitary command "would worsen considerably the situation in the Baltic region and Northern Europe." The Danish government should abstain from such action, which would "create a tense and dangerous situation there and directly concern the security of the Soviet Union."

The Danish government, however, chose to proceed with the reorganization as planned and did not answer the Soviet note until a month later. Denmark did not deny the right of the Soviet government to register its opinion on these changes in the NATO structure, but it argued against the main Soviet points. The reorganization would not unify German and Danish troops; it would only give these forces a unitary command in time of war. It was not a bilateral agreement between Denmark and the FRG, but a part of the military command structure of NATO, and therefore there was no possibility of German dominance. Denmark in any case would retain the authority to decide when and in what way its military forces would be used, including troops put under the unitary command.

Moscow stepped up its attack after NATO announced the reorganization in the beginning of December. A Soviet government declaration referred to earlier warnings, given "with the right of a good neighbor," that concessions to West German militarists would not only undermine Denmark's own security but would worsen the situation in Northern Europe and pose a threat to the countries in the Baltic area. The action taken by

Denmark "will encourage former Hitler generals and admirals in their aggressive efforts . . ., permit the penetration by West German militarists into Northern Europe and the Baltic area which will convert this traditionally peaceful region to a nest of intrigues and military preparations . . ., contribute to turning it into a military stronghold for aggression against the Soviet Union . . ., render difficult the position of Denmark's neutral neighbors." The Soviet government concluded by stating that it would be forced "to take the necessary counter-action to safeguard the security of its own country and of its allies." The Danish reply, two days later, only confirmed earlier positions.

Moscow had promised to act, but its options were limited. The Nordic link lay close at hand, demonstrative but safe. Accordingly, a Soviet note was sent to Finland on 31 October 1961 proposing consultations under the joint treaty. The Danish (and Norwegian) issue was specifically mentioned. These Soviet pressures on Helsinki are discussed below. They did not change Danish or Norwegian policy, nor could such hopes have been reasonably entertained. Perhaps, however, a link to the NATO issue would show all Nordic countries the seriousness of the situation and give a warning for the future not to alter the military status quo in the area.

Norway had its share of bilateral problems with the U.S.S.R. during this period. The expanding role of the German navy in the defense of the Baltic approaches, including portions of southern Norway, entailed stationing a few West German officers from the NATO staff at Kolsas and stockpiling fuel and ammunition for the use of the German vessels. Those arrangements evoked Soviet allegations that foreign bases were being set up which would have negative consequences for Norwegian security. While Moscow conducted its attack on Danish policies, its criticism of Norway was muted. Concurrent actions against the two Scandinavian NATO members are rare; the tactic seems to be to avoid forging the two together.

A much more awkward episode occurred in 1960, when the American U-2 spy plane was shot down over Soviet territory, an incident which became a major international crisis. It soon turned out that its destination was the Bodo airfield in northern Norway and that it was not the first such flight.

Norwegian protestations of innocence and even ignorance were rejected by Moscow, which could now claim both that this proved its constant argument that the Americans did whatever they wanted in Norway with or without Oslo's permission and that Norwegian base policy was being undermined. Soviet leaders threatened to "obliterate" the bases of aircraft which violated Soviet territory and stressed that full responsibility for complicity would rest on Norway in such cases. A few months later, when an American RB-47 spy plane was shot down over Soviet territory near Archangelsk, the Russians returned to the charge. The Russians said that although the plane had departed from a British airfield, and not a Norwegian one, it had been instructed to use Norwegian facilities in case of need. This was, the Russians said, complicity in a new and clear violation of Soviet territory for which Oslo would be held fully responsible. In this case, however, the Norwegians claimed total innocence and rejected the Soviet accusations.

The effect of this and other threats was ambiguous. On one hand, the Norwegians, displaying annoyance with Washington, professed an ardent desire to improve relations with the U.S.S.R. On the other hand, the government in Oslo found Soviet indignation somewhat excessive and reminded Moscow that increased pressure might require Norway to reconsider its policies of restraint.

Swedish-Soviet relations around 1960 contained no new bilateral complications, but they were negatively colored by various international events. Khrushchev's massive attack on Swedish U.N. Secretary General Hammarskjold must have influenced contacts between Stockholm and Moscow. Relations had already been complicated some time earlier by Soviet indignation over the awarding of the Nobel Prize to Pasternak, who was forced to refuse it. The Russians are notoriously unable to understand that the prize is given by the Swedish Academy, a private body, and not by the Swedish government, and that it is awarded on the basis of literary, not political, criteria. Long-standing Swedish support for German reunification was dealt a strong blow by the erection of the Berlin wall, which in Scandinavia, as everywhere, became a highly emotional symbol for a repressive and dictatorial system. Swedish public opinion, historically anti-Russian, was not made any more sympathetic by the nuclear mega-bomb test in Novaya Zemlya in 1961, which spread radioactive clouds throughout the Northern Hemisphere. Prime Minister Erlander's appeal to Khrushchev not to conduct this test was rudely rebuffed with the message that American armament efforts did not seem to call forth corresponding Swedish protests. Stockholm was further criticized for neglecting and even unofficially abetting the new and dangerous German militarism, an accusation that was to reappear in a later diplomatic offensive against Finland.

THE NUCLEAR ISSUE

Atomic weapons in Scandinavia became a problem in relation to the Soviet Union after the mid-1950s. Soviet interests lay principally in preventing the Scandinavian NATO partners from being linked to a chain of Western nuclear bases. Moscow applied pressure on the Scandinavians to dissuade them from acquiring nuclear weapons, and also included them in a general campaign against NATO plans to equip forces in Western Europe, including West Germany, with such arms. At the same time, a buildup of both short- and medium-range nuclear weapons was taking place in Soviet armed forces.

Three problems in Soviet-Nordic relations were raised during these years. The first concerned the implications for Scandinavia of an American offer in early 1957 to equip NATO forces with tactical nuclear weapons and dual-use short-range missiles. The second related to the American proposal in December 1957 to establish NATO stockpiles of atomic ammunition for tactical use in Europe and to give medium-range ballistic missiles to the NATO Supreme Commander in Europe (SACEUR). The third concerned discussions in the West about NATO as an independent nuclear power and on the creation of a multilateral nuclear force (MLF) which would give West Germany some control over the use of nuclear force by the Alliance.

In the mid-1950s, the NATO council authorized the military authorities to develop plans for the early use of tactical nuclear weapons in a European war. In early 1957, Washington offered to deliver short-range missiles to certain NATO countries. In the case of Norway and Denmark, one Nike (surface-to-air) missile battalion and one Honest John (surface-to-surface) missile battalion were to be set up. Both types of missiles would be adapted for dual use (that is, with or without atomic warheads).

The Soviets demonstrated concern over this buildup of nuclear-strike capability. A campaign was started to head off plans to place nuclear weapons at the disposal of NATO forces in Europe, particularly those in Germany. The Soviets made a multitude of proposals, including a nuclear test ban and the creation of a nuclear-free zone in Central Europe. Warnings were given not only to small countries but also to the U.K. and West Germany that nuclear bases on their territory could provoke preemptive strikes that would leave them no chance of survival.

As part of this campaign Bulganin wrote to his Danish (and, in somewhat milder terms, his Norwegian) counterpart. The note began with a statement that the military preparations of the North Atlantic bloc were attracting special Soviet attention. What followed was an example of the most virulent Soviet accusations and threats that have been used officially by Moscow against its Nordic neighbors in postwar times. Gone was the warm and relaxed atmosphere of the Scandinavian visits to Moscow only a year before. It was clear that the Russians had decided that threats, not blandishments, were to be used against the Scandinavians, as well; that fear, not confidence, would achieve better results in important security matters.

In the note, Bulganin first described Denmark's situation and policies. Greenland had been turned over to the U.S. as a military base outside of Danish sovereignty. "The European part of Denmark is covered by a net of military airports and marine bases, built according to NATO military command plans, where American and British instructors are active. Thus no guarantee exists that foreign forces, called in by NATO command, would not appear on a few hours' notice on these Danish bases to be used against peace-loving countries. . . . NATO great powers can very well start military operations without giving their small allies any advance notice." Thus recurred the general theme that Denmark, whatever its pacific intentions, would be fully exploited by its more powerful partners if it gave in to their early demands.

Bulganin then turned to the matter at hand, "the plans to put special American units, equipped with nuclear weapons, on Danish territory." "The Soviet government does not wish to paint in strong colors, but let me tell you, without any ado, that Denmark, by being implicated in the military preparations of certain powers, runs a very serious and indefensible risk. . . . The Soviet people have no wish that the U.S.S.R., Denmark, or any other country be the target of an atomic bombardment or feel the effects of other modern weapons. But . . . the Soviet government would be remiss in its duty if it did not, in response to aggression, take immediate steps to direct a crushing blow against the aggressor and his whole net of military strongholds and bases established to attack the Soviet Union. . . . The devastating power of modern weapons is so great that in an atomic war, it would be tantamount to suicide for a country the size of Denmark to have given bases to foreign powers." By dwelling even further on the large-scale effects of these modern weapons, Bulganin did his best to bring home his point.

But atomic weapons were not the only issue. Two other points close to the hearts of Soviet policy makers--the straits and Danish neutrality--were thrown in by Bulganin, as though the whole security relationship could be dealt with once and for all. "Denmark is the guardian of important international straits, and all Baltic nations are dependent on these for their normal shipping and, in some part, for the security of their populations." This imposed a special responsibility on the Danish government. NATO was interested in Denmark mainly because it occupied a position controlling exit from and entry to the Baltic. A policy which linked Denmark's fate to a specific military power group was not a very wise one. "Would it not be much more useful for Denmark . . . to seek its security in international guarantees for its independence and territorial integrity. . . ?"

The Danes chose to respond in a polite but general manner to this outburst, arguing mainly about the defensive nature of NATO and about the Danish policy of never letting its territory be used for aggression. The government did, however, declare its intention to accept American offers of short-range missiles (the Nike and the Honest John), but to refuse atomic warheads "under present conditions." In response to later American proposals made after the launch of the Russian Sputnik, Denmark declared that it would not accept atomic ammunition or installations for medium-range missiles on its territory. In explaining this policy, the Danish government specifically referred to Soviet reactions and to Denmark's need not to act provocatively or increase tension in the sensitive Nordic region.

The Norwegians received similar communications from Bulganin. Norway's prime minister announced that Norway "had no plans to let atomic stockpiles be established on Norwegian territory or to construct launching sites for IRBMs."

Bulganin signed several new letters on the subject. While expressing satisfaction over these Scandinavian decisions, he pointed out that airfields in Denmark and Norway were being equipped to receive long-range bombers able to carry nuclear weapons, and that these countries also were to receive short-range missiles, which, like any other missiles, could be equipped with nuclear warheads. It would no doubt be an even better contribution to peace and stability in the North if Denmark took a position "which made it impossible for atomic weapons or missiles to be put on Danish territory." A corresponding decision by Norway would, given the position of Finland and Sweden, "create preconditions for making the whole of Northern

Europe into a zone free of atomic and fire weapons, an important guarantee for peace and stability in the area" (Bulganin, 12 December 1957 and 8 January 1958).

It is worth noting that neither the Danes nor the Norwegians, in any direct message to Moscow, undertook to refrain from nuclear weapons. Their policies were stated within NATO or in national contexts. They rejected Soviet criticism of short-range tactical missiles for dual use, and the question whether to equip these missiles with nuclear warheads at some later stage was not decided at this juncture. By retaining the right to review their positions at any time and by refusing to assign legal status to their current policies, Norway and Denmark denied the Soviet Union any right to interpret their positions or any *droit de regard* on their policies.

The nuclear problem was a hot internal political issue in both Norway and Denmark during this period, and the discussions and the outcome were similar. Norwegian military authorities proposed in 1960 that tactical nuclear weapons should form a part of Norway's defense and that, therefore, such weapons should be stockpiled in peacetime. The government, however, decided that, while such weapons might very well be brought into the country by Allied troops in wartime, they should not be stationed there in peacetime. The spread of nuclear weapons should generally be prevented. Norway, as a neighbor of the Soviet Union, was in a particularly sensitive position and also had to see to it that tensions were not increased in Northern Europe. That decision, even though it was coupled with an increase in conventional defense outlays, probably soothed relations with Moscow, which had been recently soured by the U-2 affair and discussions of Norwegian policy regarding NATO bases.

Norway, and to a lesser extent Denmark, was skeptical of U.S. proposals in 1962-63 for an interallied nuclear force, and even more skeptical of proposals for a multilateral nuclear force. Both nations wanted America to retain its monopoly on nuclear weapons; neither nation wanted a West German finger on the trigger, particularly since this was bound to provoke the

Russians. They stated that the spread of nuclear weapons to non-nuclear states should be prevented, and that they would not themselves be a part of any such force. They reiterated their positions banning nuclear weapons on their own territories, and the Danish government specified, in reference to NATO submarines with Polaris nuclear-tipped missiles, that the ban applied also to Danish waters and ports. The Norwegians, likewise, stated that "no NATO naval units with nuclear weapons would be allowed to establish themselves in Norwegian waters in peacetime." The Soviet Union had firmly objected to the MLF/ANF projects. It took note of the Scandinavian countries' stand but remained skeptical about real intentions in Copenhagen and Oslo, perhaps as part of a strategem to further push the Scandinavians into accepting the plan for a Nordic nuclear-free zone, proposed by Finland's President Kekkonen in 1963.

The Swedes, too, engaged in internal debate from the late 1950s to the mid-1960s over whether to equip the armed forces with nuclear weapons for use in the battlefield. Moscow refrained from any direct official intervention in this debate, although it revealed its distaste in press articles describing efforts by "reactionary elements and militarists" to link Sweden to NATO's nuclear planning. Moscow emphasized that the credibility of Swedish neutrality would be undermined by the purchase of such weapons or of delivery vehicles for them. Swedish nuclear weapons would be incompatible with neutrality, principally because they would create links to the Western powers. Soviet media clearly hinted that countries--neutral or not--that possessed such weapons would be the first to receive massive strikes if a war broke out. Their nuclear weapons, rather than contributing significantly to defense, would instead only invite total destruction at an early stage. This was strange reasoning, since, apart from some initial proposals by the military to acquire some limited "strategic" capability--proposals that were quickly rejected--the Swedes had talked exclusively about battlefield weapons which would only be used defensively against the armed forces of an aggressor. Although "defensive use" in some military planning circles seemed to include attacks against Soviet ports in the Baltic used for troop transport, the Soviet threats seemed excessive. The Russians were no doubt concerned principally about the possible spread of nuclear weapons--a process which could be influenced by the Swedish decision--and wanted to intimate dire consequences. Incidentally, their negative attitude toward Swedish atomic weapons was fully shared in Washington.

Although the Swedes were not overly influenced by these great-power comments, they decided after a lively internal debate that it would be better to rely upon a strong conventional defense and they pursued their very sizeable efforts to maintain such a force. Five generations of indigenous jet aircraft were constructed, and 5 percent of GNP was devoted to defense until the early 1970s, when that figure leveled off to between 3.5 percent and 3.0 percent.

While Soviet attitudes toward large Swedish defense outlays have been consistently negative, a much more aggressive line would no doubt have been taken if the Swedes had decided to acquire nuclear weapons.

A RETURN TO FINLAND: THE NIGHT FROST OF 1958 AND THE NOTE CRISIS OF 1961

There is no indication that the renewed tension in Europe and in the relations with the Scandinavians was the source of Soviet pressure on Finland at the end of the 1950s. On the contrary, both Moscow and Helsinki had been anxious to ensure that international conflicts or other outside events not influence their good relations with each other. The chill that set in in the late 1950s was clearly bilateral, a function of Soviet ambitions to influence Finland's internal politics.

In the autumn of 1958, the Soviet ambassador in Helsinki left his post without the usual ceremonies, and no successor was appointed. Moscow imposed a freeze on a number of unfinished bilateral negotiations, explaining that it was dissatisfied with the composition of the new Finnish government, which it said was dominated by anti-Soviet Social Democrats and Conservatives, and with certain negative trends in Finnish public opinion. Khrushchev scathingly accused Finnish newspapers of "rummaging in the dust bin of history" to find material to worsen relations with the U.S.S.R. Suggestions to revise the border, books about forced labor camps in Russia, and memoirs about Comintern intrigues were cited as examples. Clearly, Moscow thought that the Finns had become dizzy with the Porkkala success. In the meantime, Finland's trade had gradually shifted back toward its traditional commercial partners in the West, and Finnish industrial and business circles were promoting plans for a Nordic common market or for participation in a larger West European free-trade area.

The most important issue, however, was Soviet suspicion of Social Democratic party leaders Tanner and Leskinen, who were both regarded as foes of communism. Tanner was considered the arch-villain and held responsible for the war against the Soviet Union. Right-wing Social Democrats had now formed a government in alliance with conservative parties, even though the Communists had made their best showing ever in an election and become the biggest single party in parliament and among the electorate, albeit with a small margin and in a splintered party situation.

Khrushchev had no problem in making it clear to the Finns that the government, as it was composed, would have great problems in relations with Moscow. It was soon succeeded by a minority agrarian party government. President Kekkonen, meeting Khrushchev in Leningrad, was assured that the issue for Moscow had in fact been "those persons behind the prime minister (Fagerholm) well-known for their hostility toward the Soviet Union" and the anti-Soviet publicity. Now that these problems had been solved, all sanctions could be lifted. The crisis was thus short-lived, but it betrayed a Soviet sensitivity to internal Finnish politics, which in contrast to 1948 met no strong resistance in Helsinki. Various political forces in Finland stood to gain from the failure of the new government. Considerable debate has focused on whether "the Soviet card" was overplayed in the internal power game, but the decisive manner in which the Russians proceeded with concurrent diplomatic and economic sanctions made it clear that any solution must take their interests into account.

Three years later, a far more serious crisis surfaced which was closely linked to Nordic and European issues. In a note delivered on 30 October 1961, Moscow requested consultations with Finland under the terms of the Treaty on Friendship, Cooperation, and Mutual Assistance which refer to threats from "Germany or countries allied with Germany."

European and global tensions formed the background to the crisis. The main Soviet preoccupation seemed to be the political and military rise of West Germany, particularly the danger that it might acquire control over nuclear weapons. Moscow's horizon was also clouded by the expansion of American strategic forces and by increased trouble with China. In the summer of 1961, Moscow and Washington escalated their rhetoric concerning military preparations, and the Russians soon decided to resume nuclear testing, breaking the ban that had been adhered to for several years. Moscow also announced its intention to raise the issue of Berlin and to press the question of a German peace treaty. American troops and equipment were transported to Europe and, as part of the flexible response strategy that was being adopted, a considerable increase in the conventional strength of the Western Alliance was undertaken.

There have been various interpretations of Soviet motives behind the note crisis. Some analysts have claimed that the initiative was a direct outgrowth of the Berlin issue, intended to dramatize Soviet willpower in a safe way. The Berlin crisis no doubt colored Moscow's general foreign policy at this time, but it did not relate directly to Finland. The peak of that crisis had passed when the Soviets proposed consultations with the Finns. The erection of the Berlin wall on 13 August signaled the beginning of a Soviet retreat from intentions to conclude a treaty with East Germany and push the Berlin question to a truly dangerous point.

Others have pointed to internal tension in Moscow, as evidenced by the differences in the tones of speeches by various officials at the 22nd Party Congress assembled on 17 October. Khrushchev was relatively restrained in comparison with his earlier pronouncements; Gromyko "preached" for U.S.-Soviet rapproachment, whereas Marshal Malinovsky used much more bellicose language, claiming with heavy irony that Soviet long-range missiles possessed splendid accuracy. The initiative toward Finland could have been either a victory for the hardliners or a concession made to assuage them. Indeed, the later discussions between the Finns and the Russians revealed some conflicts within the Soviet leadership and indicated that the military were more trigger-happy than the civilians. However, although differences were there, it is unlikely that the Finnish issue figured prominently in the power struggle in the Kremlin given the many more important matters on the agenda. Still other analysts have seen the Soviet initiative as a way of influencing the upcoming Finnish presidential election.

All these factors might well have contributed to the Soviet decision. Clearly, however, Nordic security problems linked to NATO plans and, above all, West German rearmament were uppermost in Moscow's mind in making the Finnish initiative. The note stressed the dangerous situation prevailing in the Baltic, the increased West German influence in Norway and Denmark, and Sweden's "tendency to underestimate the danger of West German military preparations in Northern Europe and willingness to cooperate with that country." The note repeated, almost verbatim, assertions published earlier in a Soviet periodical (A. Pogodin in *International Affairs*, 1961, p. 9). The article referred to the rapid growth of the West German navy in the Baltic, rumors about Bonn's plans to equip its Baltic fleet with Polaris missiles, joint military exercises by German, Danish, and Norwegian troops, and, above all, plans to establish a joint Danish-German military command for army, navy, and air force units in Denmark, Schleswig-Holstein, and the Baltic. All this "proved" West German intentions to achieve dominance in the western Baltic and to establish bases in Norway and

Denmark. This, it seems, was regarded by Moscow as a "threat of military aggression" as defined in the treaty on consultations.

No complaint was lodged against Finland's official policies. Indeed, during a visit to Finland only a month earlier, President Brezhnev had spoken of "the peaceful foreign policy which has been consistently followed by President Kekkonen and Finland's government." In the note, this policy was contrasted to "certain circles in Finland [that] actively support the dangerous military preparations of the member states of NATO and contribute . . . to the dissemination of war psychosis."

Tass followed up a few days later (6 November 1961) in the same vein--benevolent toward Finland, positive but skeptical about Sweden. Sweden's nonaligned policy could certainly promote peace in Europe, but that policy was undermined by some political circles in Sweden which held positive attitudes toward Bonn's aggressive plans, particularly in the Baltic region. Although Norway and Denmark themselves had no aggressive plans, they encouraged the West German military, creating a threat on the Soviet-Finnish borders.

The Finns reacted calmly, in contrast to the Swedish and international press. Kekkonen, vacationing in Hawaii, indicated that the government had not yet decided whether consultations were necessary, implying that consultations, according to the treaty, had to be agreed to by both parties, and not simply decreed by Moscow. The Finns wanted to avoid, or at least to delay, consultations in which military measures would have to be discussed. To that end, the Finnish foreign minister went to Moscow to meet with Gromyko, who introduced a new aspect. "The political situation in Finland has become unstable and there is in Finland a certain political grouping whose purpose is to prevent the continuation of the present foreign policy orientation. . . . The Soviet government is willing to accept immediate assurances that Finland's present foreign policy orientation will continue and that nothing will prevent the development of friendly relations between Finland and the Soviet Union. If this kind of certainty can be obtained very soon, military consultations can perhaps be avoided" (Gromyko on 11 November as quoted in a Finnish government communique on 14 November 1961).

This was clearly a new perspective. Up to this point, the issue had been the West German/Danish angle. However, Finnish internal politics were also of great interest to the Russians. Presidential elections were to be held in 1962. Kekkonen's opponent, Honka, had support from Social Democrats and Conservatives, who were both regarded with great suspicion in Moscow. Soviet media had for some time criticized Honka while expressing total confidence in the incumbent Kekkonen.

Gromyko's opinion, however, was soon "overruled." A few days later, his deputy reverted to the original theme--the sharpening military crisis in the region--and requested in a conversation with the Finnish ambassador in Moscow that negotiations be started as soon as possible. He cited three reasons in particular: a visit to Norway by West German Defense Minister Franz Josef Strauss, NATO naval exercises in the western part of the Baltic Sea, and the unitary command. Gromyko had mentioned to his Finnish counterpart that the Soviet military had been demanding for some time that consultations should be started. It now seemed that they would have it their way.

Kekkonen decided to discuss the matter personally with Khrushchev and was received in Novosibirsk on 24 November. He argued that, while Soviet perceptions of the dangers of war were no doubt highly significant, consultations under the treaty would very likely cause a war-panic in Scandinavia which would have negative effects for all concerned. Khrushchev had, in fact, just been visited by the Norwegian foreign minister, who had expressed Oslo's deep concern and hinted at possible negative effects on Norway's nuclear or base policies should pressure on Finland continue. Moreover, the Soviets were at this time attempting to de-escalate the Berlin crisis. It was agreed, then, that the Finnish-Soviet negotiations could be postponed. The Soviet leader, who was probably not too keen to add Finland to his many troubles or to embark upon consultations that would upset the Nordic situation, seemed to soften his position in his outline of the two strands of thought that had led to Moscow's initiative.

On one hand, he stressed that Finland should follow events in Northern Europe and, if necessary, express its views on measures that would promote peace. Presumably, this included Finnish opinions on the issue at hand, the NATO naval buildup in the Baltic. It was thus implied that the Finns should express themselves according to their own judgment but with the understanding that Finnish security interests in Northern Europe often ran parallel to those of the Soviet Union. Kekkonen emphasized the other side of that coin, namely, that Finland and not the Soviet Union had been given primary responsibility for asking for consultations under the treaty, if they thought it necessary.

Khrushchev, however, also stressed "that the action of rightist and Tannerist groups in Finland, aiming to destroy the friendship between the Soviet Union and Finland and to break the Paasikivi-Kekkonen line, causes serious uneasiness with us." The reference to the presidential elections was clear and it got the intended result: Honka withdrew from the race. The Soviet concern about the threat posed by Honka might have been misplaced, however, since he had little chance of winning anyway.

The Russians, some of whom were no doubt more trigger-happy than others, were interested primarily in reminding both the Finns and the Scandinavian NATO members of the need for political caution in dangerous times. The effect on the latter was, at best, ambiguous. The Danes, as expected, went ahead with the NATO project for a unitary command in the Baltic, but they had been given food for thought. The Norwegians reacted to the pressure on Helsinki by talking about possible further integration into NATO and hinting vaguely about modifications to Norway's nuclear policies. The Swedes, whose special concern had for once been recognized by Moscow, which had contacted them early on, chose to publicly reaffirm their belief that Moscow would do nothing to change Finland's neutral status, and wisely rejected American proposals to more actively support Helsinki. Swedish policy, said Prime Minister Erlander, would be "not to compromise our neutrality in any way and not to do anything that can injure Finland's interests."

Since the note crisis until the present time, the Soviets have refrained from overt pressure on the Finns. A general consensus evolved in Finland on its foreign policy line and its requirements. Moscow, for its part, has lifted the ban on the Social Democratic and Conservative parties while watching carefully and pressuring gently to promote its own political favorites.

Kekkonen's foreign policy initiatives, both before and after the note crisis, have met with Soviet approval for the most part, even though their principal aims have no doubt been to satisfy Finnish security and political interests. A nuclear-free zone in the North would eliminate the risk that the Soviet Union would choose to invoke the Finnish-Soviet treaty over Norwegian-Danish discussions on atomic weapons. A pact between Norway and Finland to pacify the Finnish-Norwegian border, the most sensitive part of Northern Europe, would likewise serve to calm Moscow on this front and delay the implementation of the 1948 treaty provisions. A general neutralization of Northern Europe could place Finland in a reasonably secure Nordic grouping. Criticism in early 1965 of West German participation in a multilateral nuclear force (MLF), when the MLF project had already been scrapped, seemed to indicate both understanding of Soviet positions and awareness that Western sensitivity to critical neutral opinions on their strategic arrangements would then, presumably, be fairly low.

Also in 1965, Kekkonen went out of his way to dismiss as wholly unrealistic proposals for a Nordic defense union that would include Finland (which then would have to repudiate the FCMA treaty), neutral Sweden, and Norway and Denmark (which would have to leave NATO). Finland had no wish whatsoever to abandon its 1948 treaty with the Soviet Union.

Khrushchev soon expressed new interest in a visit to Scandinavia to improve relations. The biggest spy incident in Swedish-Soviet relations, the Wennerstrom case, came to light in

June 1963, but it did not prevent the arrival of the Soviet leader one year later. A third cancellation would indeed have been awkward for both parties. The trip, Khrushchev's next-to-last foreign visit before his fall from power a few months later, produced no substantial results, but it did serve to solidify a Scandinavian-Soviet relationship that from then until recent times has been less problematic and eventful.

Khrushchev took the opportunity while in Oslo to outline his ideal for the Nordic countries in a speech, which, typically, also contained some veiled threats: "From our point of view, countries like Norway, Denmark, Sweden, and Finland could best guarantee their security by adopting a policy of neutrality recognized by both parties--the Western powers as well as the socialist countries. Such a policy would guarantee that these countries, in case of military conflict, would be protected from the devastating effects of modern weapons."

Chapter 3

RELAXATION, STABILITY, AND TENSION: THE PAST TWENTY-FIVE YEARS

Until the early 1960s, relations between the Soviet Union and the Nordic countries, although considerably less tense than general East-West relations, were still strained by harsh Soviet criticism, angry messages, and easy suspicions. The next twenty years, until the end of the 1970s, were on the whole calmer and more stable.

One important reason for this stability was the relaxation of international tension that began after the Cuban missile crisis and peaked in the early 1970s, to be followed by a gradual return to more frosty relations. The focus of tension, too, shifted from Europe to Indochina, the Middle East, and Africa. A second reason was the change of political leadership in Moscow in 1964, when the ebullient Khrushchev, prone to brinkmanship and dramatic gestures, was succeeded by a prudent and more carefully pragmatic collective group. While the character of the group and its style did not change over the years, succession problems, long rule, and old age might have lessened its grip on all aspects of foreign affairs. The new leadership that came to power in early 1985 in Moscow clearly is in firm command of foreign policy. While, understandably, it has so far not devoted much attention to the Nordic area, general attitudes do not reveal any signs of change.

A third factor is related to the Soviet arms buildup and the resulting change in the global balance of power since the mid-1960s. Moscow has been able to act with more confidence--less fearful of NATO moves in Europe, more activist in the Third World--in the awareness of strategic parity with the United States. One can speculate whether this ability has gradually given the military, the most successful and prestigious group in Soviet society, a larger say in the business of the state or more independence within its own sphere of activity. It seems clear, however, that the top Soviet military have become more firmly subordinated to the civilian party leadership in the post-Brezhnev era (since November 1982) than they were under Brezhnev. American and Western military decisions (INF deployment, cruise missile development, etc.) in response to the Soviet buildup have probably enhanced the position of those in Moscow who argue for a forceful though prudent posture in Europe and preparation for any eventuality.

The Soviet military might indeed be more inclined than the civilian leadership to retain the two-camps mentality, viewing all of Scandinavia as potentially hostile or at least open to enemy exploitation. The general Soviet belief that small capitalist countries with a Western orientation will easily fall prey to American schemes is difficult to dispel. Neutrality, although accepted and appreciated politically, fits only with difficulty into a military mind-set.

A fourth, and not the least important, explanation for the relative but certainly not complete serenity in the Nordic area is that the political and military patterns there became fairly well established in the early 1960s and have remained so. Since 1961, Finland has gained the confidence of Moscow to a degree it obviously had not achieved prior to that time. Practically all Finnish parties across the political spectrum are now deemed trustworthy by Moscow.

Sweden's policies have been seen by Moscow's political leaders as on the whole positive.

Denmark and Norway established their base and nuclear policies, although particularly in Norway's case these policies have been continually challenged by Moscow in an effort to narrow Norway's margins for maneuver. Soviet leaders have repeatedly referred to Norwegian and Danish membership in

NATO as "a misunderstanding" or "an anomaly." Khrushchev's statement in 1964 during a visit to Norway still remains Soviet policy: "A neutral status for all the Nordic countries with international recognition would be the best policy for their peoples and for peace."

Soviet attention to the Scandinavian NATO members increased when their security policy was under debate, e.g., in connection with the decision to remain in NATO in 1969. Soviet ambivalence toward a Scandinavian defense alliance was repeatedly demonstrated. On 10 September 1966, *Izvestija* attacked the concept, repeating that neutrality, guaranteed by the great powers, was a sufficient and useful alternative to NATO. But only a month later, on 20 October, the same paper stated that a Scandinavian alliance was a "possible alternative," provided it stayed outside existing military blocs. This latter position has since disappeared from Soviet commentary.

A more permanent feature in Soviet analyses of the Nordic security situation has been the negative stand taken toward the concept of a "Nordic balance." This is an idea which postulates an "equilibrium" between, on one hand, Norwegian, Danish, and Icelandic NATO membership with their restrictions, and, on the other hand, Finland's special relationship to the U.S.S.R., with Sweden being placed somewhere in the middle. A change in one part of the system would have a direct bearing on other parts. It is easy to understand why the Russians dislike the idea. Decreased NATO presence in Scandinavia should for example entail a change in Finland's status away from the Soviet Union! Moscow also dislikes the thought that its relations with Finland should at all be linked to its standing in other parts of the North. The negative Soviet attitude toward this concept is shared by the Finns, who object to having their relations with the U.S.S.R. put on a par with Norwegian and Danish NATO membership. The concept of a "Nordic balance," which was fairly prevalent in Scandinavia in the 1950s and early 1960s, has also receded very much to the background, partly in response to the stabilization of Finnish-Soviet relations.

In the 1980s, Soviet-Nordic relations have varied more. Finland has enjoyed fairly serene coexistence with her neighbor, despite the ups and downs of the international climate. Denmark, a frequent dissenter in NATO councils and lax in its own defense efforts, gets fairly positive treatment. Norway, however, is increasingly accused of integrating itself into the Western military camp and thus posing problems for the security of Soviet strategic interests in the far North. Indeed, NATO military presence in Denmark and Norway has increased in recent years, although at the same time there has been a growing political trend toward a non-nuclear policy, not only in peacetime but also in crises and perhaps even in war.

Sweden, officially lauded and cultivated for many years as an almost exemplary neutral neighbor, has been the object of Soviet submarine intrusions in recent years. The subsequent increase of tension in the relationship has been marked by the resurrection of old or hidden Swedish sins in Moscow's propaganda.

Thus, there is no clear relationship between the level of international tension and Nordic-Soviet bilateral conflicts. The changing strategic context in the North, as well as specific internal or external political factors, must be taken into account to arrive at a good explanation of this recent pattern.

A reasonable hypothesis would be that Soviet policy regarding the Nordic area--a group of stable, reasonably amicable, and above all prudent countries--is one, not of great top-level attention, but of positive vigilance combined with steady pressure in order to maintain and, if possible, improve a fairly satisfactory situation and to insure against any negative developments arising from internal or external sources. Let us test this hypothesis against the available evidence contained in the Soviet media, official declarations, and actual behavior, and also try to gauge Soviet military interests in a changing strategic context.

FINLAND

Finnish-Soviet relations were consistently hailed by Moscow as "a symbol of peaceful coexistence" and as proof that one superpower at least could entertain friendly and unobtrusive cooperation with a small neighbor. The Treaty on Friendship, Cooperation, and Mutual Assistance (FCMA) contained such principles, said Brezhnev, that were later to be introduced in the Helsinki accord on European security and cooperation. Finland was highly praised for its role as an active proponent of various peace initiatives in the Nordic area, Europe, and globally. Finnish leaders, alone outside of the socialist camp, maintained regular and frequent contact with Moscow's top decision makers, and consultations on all levels have become a regular practice. The Khrushchev-Kekkonen relationship was unique and fruitful. Among the troika that took office in 1964, Kosygin became the principal partner to the Finnish president. Brezhnev, the party general secretary who around 1970 established his primacy in foreign affairs, never visited Finland in that capacity. While this group was presumably not willing to subscribe to Khrushchev's 1960 assertion that "as long as Kekkonen leads Finland we trust it even with our eyes closed," the Finnish leader still inspired much confidence and respect in Moscow. A significant gesture, for example, was Kosygin's special visit to Finland in October 1968 to explain to the irate and disappointed Kekkonen why Moscow had found it necessary to invade Czechoslovakia. The Soviet leader could then perhaps concur with the Finnish president's view that Moscow had far more trouble with its allies than with friendly, neutral--and capitalist--Finland.

The need for such close contacts has been demonstrated by occasional problems even in quiet and peaceful periods. Some circles in the U.S.S.R. seem to take a more restrictive view of Finnish autonomy and have at times been fairly vociferous. Leningrad and Karelia might house activists such as these, who have close links with the Stalinist faction of the Finnish Communists and who seem to enjoy better access in Moscow than in Khrushchevian times. Opinions might also differ between the military and the civilians in the Soviet hierarchy. There is no longer any "lobbyist" for Finland in the Kremlin (like Mikoyan and Kosygin) nor anyone with a special knowledge of that country. Perhaps a need no longer exists for that kind of support.

Moscow no doubt gave much thought to the Finnish presidential election in early 1982, since Kekkonen, after twenty-five years in office, was to retire. Soviet media reminded readers that, while anti-Soviet forces in Finland had decreased in importance, they were still influential. Before the election, an article in *Pravda* stated:

> The forces that supported Kekkonen and his for-
> eign policy course bear particularly great respon-
> sibility. Any miscalculation that they make in
> approaching the question of whose hands shall re-
> ceive Kekkonen's political legacy may lead to
> consequences which are difficult to foretell.

Moscow clearly had its own favorites (Karjalainen of Kekkonen's Centre party) which it tried to promote, but the pressure was gentle and no heavy-handed means were used, even when other candidates were chosen. The Social Democrat, Koivisto, was elected and received positive but prudently worded congratulations from Brezhnev. The new Finnish leader visited Moscow six weeks after the election. He obviously showed great prudence so as not to be seen as a supporter of Soviet positions. In the communique there was thus a complete absence of any even veiled criticism of Norwegian policies, although *Pravda* the day before had lambasted the bourgeois government in Norway for its pro-NATO policies. A year later, Koivisto once again visited Moscow, where he was now greeted by Andropov as a leader "in the line of Paasikivi and Kekkonen." The communique from this meeting reiterated Brezhnev's 1980 statements on ways and means of avoiding conflicts in the North (see below).

Events in the Nordic region affected Soviet-Finnish relations in various ways. Meeting with Nordic prime ministers in Helsinki in 1977, Kosygin attacked Norway for its military cooperation with NATO countries, and specifically with West Germany. Voronkov and other Soviet commentators sometimes expounded the theory that the risks of war in the Nordic area, and thus the need to invoke the military part of the FCMA treaty, would be decreased if Norway and Denmark (and Iceland) pulled out of NATO, which would also ease the way to the establishment of a nuclear-free zone.

When President Kekkonen visited Moscow in November 1980, Norway had just decided to stockpile NATO equipment (see below). On 11 August, *Pravda* had claimed that "all NATO's militaristic programs to be implemented in and around Northern Europe are directed against the Soviet Union and directly threaten the Swedes' and the Finns' security." Brezhnev did not go that far in his dinner speeches, but he stressed that "the security of the European north can be ensured not by the stepped-up activity of military blocs, but by a joint search for solutions that could leave this region outside the sphere of conflicts." Kekkonen used stronger words:

> Up to now, each of the Nordic countries has been accustomed in their security policy decisions to take into consideration the other Nordic countries. . . . No one's interest can be served by the upsetting of the stable situation in Northern Europe or even less by a deliberate increase in tension there. The main thing now is restraint.

The communique from the Kekkonen visit reflected these sentiments, but the final Norwegian decisions to go ahead on the matter, made a few months later, did not seem to disturb Soviet-Finnish relations. If anything, whether by Finnish or Soviet initiative, the exchange of friendly visits between Helsinki and Moscow during these troubled times in Soviet-Scandinavian relations seemed even more frequent than usual.

Finnish-Soviet relations since 1980 have been explicitly disassociated from international events, as reflected in communiques and in Soviet declarations that "the favorable development of these relations do not depend on the fluctuations in the international situation" (*Pravda-Izvestija*, 13 November 1980, and Andropov's speech in *Pravda*, 7 June 1983). Finnish-Soviet communiques have long stated that "outside events" should not impair relations, implying, for instance, that Soviet actions in Hungary, Czechoslovakia, and Afghanistan should not interrupt frequent political contacts. Linkage with Europe in general is also implicitly rejected, as in Soviet insistence that countermeasures to INF deployment in Western Europe, especially in West Germany, will be taken "with a view to the areas where these missiles are located and to the territory of the United States itself." Thus, retaliation will be considered against the *provocateurs* only. However, some Soviet comments (by Kommissarov, for instance) have referred to Kekkonen's warnings about the dire implications for Finnish security posed by NATO cruise missiles aimed at the Soviet Union. These comments have intimated that cruise missiles to be fired over Finnish territory might be cause to invoke the FCMA treaty. As recently as September 1984, Prime Minister Tichonov also discussed new American weapons and their possible implications for Finland.

One issue that has been discussed intermittently in Finland is the various Soviet formulae used to describe Finnish foreign policy and Finnish-Soviet relations. In 1956, Finnish "neutrality" was recognized in Khrushchev's statement to the 20th Party Congress. Since the early 1970s, "neutrality" is no longer used by Moscow to describe Finland's foreign policy. Instead, Soviet statements stress the FCMA treaty, although the Finns insist that, in their view, there is no contradiction between the treaty and Finland's neutrality. The preferred phraseology in Moscow is "a policy striving for peace and neutrality," or, echoing the treaty's preamble, "a policy striving to keep Finland out of great-power conflicts."

Along with top-level contacts and speeches, some books on relations with Finland have appeared which have stressed the military cooperation aspect of the FCMA treaty (for instance, T. Bartenyev and Y. Kommissarov, *Tridtsat let Dobrososedstva* (1976)). Although the appearance of these books did not seem to be linked to any specific international or Nordic events, they might have been a response to the theorizing on this issue that was going on in Finland. The military stipulations of the treaty "give it the character of a treaty of joint guarantees of security on a bilateral basis, a treaty on military cooperation," the authors said. The military clauses would come into force if there was a danger of a military offensive forming against the Soviet Union in Northern Europe and the Baltic Sea area. Other states in addition to Germany should be seen as main triggers of the treaty clauses. Finns should not stress their own defense measures exclusively, but should also take into account the possibility of military cooperation with the Soviet Union.

This was clearly a far-reaching interpretation of the treaty, made particularly ominous by the fact that the military-political situation in Northern Europe did indeed evolve and change during the latter part of the 1970s (discussed below). Kommissarov, said to be a pseudonym for an authoritative group in the Foreign Ministry and Central Committee in Moscow, subsequently described the first paragraph of the treaty as an "obligation to fight together against armed aggression," which was the formula used in the 1948 Soviet draft of the treaty (preface to Karvonen, *Sovetskij Sojus: Finlandija* (1977)). These and other Soviet academic studies downplay Finnish neutrality and stress Helsinki's active stance for peace. They also refer to the threat that the buildup of U.S. cruise missiles on bombers, surface ships, and submarines poses to vital installations in northwestern parts of the Soviet Union, implying (but not stating) that this might increase the need for the U.S.S.R. to extend its air defense zone in Northern Europe. Recently they have claimed repeatedly that the Pentagon and the Reagan administration clearly have plans to draw Finland toward the West and that they make great efforts to exploit anti-Soviet forces in that country.

Some commotion was created in Helsinki political circles by claims first made in Western papers that Soviet Defense Minister Ustinov, during a visit to Finland in July 1978, had unofficially suggested joint Finnish-Soviet military maneuvers in peacetime. The rumors were fueled by articles containing similar proposals in a Finnish Communist newspaper. The Finnish defense minister publicly declared, in response to a question in parliament, that the contacts between the armed forces of the two countries take the form of customary exchanges of visits, as well as of equipment procurements and training:

> The FCMA treaty renders possible military cooperation between the two countries in a crisis situation precisely defined by the treaty. Peacetime joint exercises or similar cooperation in the military sphere would, however, be incompatible with Finland's international status.

The Finns denied that any official proposals had been made, but found it necessary, as they had in 1961, to add that speculation about such exercises would destabilize the situation in Northern Europe. "The government of Finland knows that the government of the Soviet Union is not endeavoring to alter the stable situation in the North."

Why did Ustinov make the proposal, as, according to Max Jakobson, a well-informed Finnish observer and a former ambassador, he indeed seems to have done? No connection was claimed or can be established between this and events in the Nordic area. Full Soviet attention was turned to Norwegian-NATO arms measures only a year later, and Oslo had just shown restraint in limiting West German participation in NATO maneuvers in northern Norway. However, the remarks, coming as they did after the Kommissarov writings, coinciding with the Communist newspaper articles, and never denied by Moscow, can hardly be considered gratuitous or flippant. Differences among Soviet decision makers over Finland have been apparent several times, but not at this level during the period of collective Kremlin leadership. There was no reason to expect anything but a thoroughly negative Finnish response, which could hardly further Soviet interests. The entire episode might have been simply another signal to the Finns not to forget Finland's special cooperative military relationship with the U.S.S.R. Subsequent events have seemed to indicate a Soviet retreat from the probings made by Ustinov and in the

Kommissarov articles. The atmosphere has since become more relaxed.

Finnish Defense

Helsinki has reasoned that a strong Finnish defense would be in the interest of both parties to the FCMA treaty. Finland wants to postpone for as long as possible, if not avoid altogether, the arrival of Soviet troops on its soil. At the same time, Finnish defense against any attacks from the West would ease a burden that otherwise could fall on Soviet forces. Finland's military capacity can be strengthened by cooperation between the two parties in such areas as the delivery of military equipment, purchases of hardware, etc.

The Soviet Union has shown a relatively positive attitude toward Finnish defense. The Paris Peace Treaty of 1947 limited standing Finnish forces to only about 42,000 men with sixty aircraft and no missiles, bombs, or submarines. In 1963, however, the Soviet Union and other signatory states agreed to changes which reflected the evolution of military technology and the need for Finland to credibly defend its neutrality. The treaty limitations are now considered to cover only the standing army, and not the training and arming of a large reserve force of 250,000 men which can be called up on short notice. Defensive missiles, mainly small Soviet ground-to-air SAM-7s and batteries of SAM-3s around Helsinki, form part of the Finnish arsenal, as does an air force of two hundred military aircraft, including MIG-21s and Swedish Drakens. In recent years, Finland has increased its land forces as well as its air bases in Finnish Lapland and has installed a well-developed system of long-distance and low-level radar installations. Lapland can thus be held, it is believed, against "realistic" challenges. Sales of Soviet equipment to Finland in fact far exceed the needs of the standing army. Because of foreign policy considerations the Finns are careful in their procurement policies and acquire approximately one-third of their equipment from the Soviet Union, one-third from the West (Sweden, the U.K., the U.S.), and one-third from their own production. Officers from both countries exchange fairly frequent courtesy visits, which might provide insights into the attitudes of the other party; the Finns, however, do not receive any instructors or advisors linked to the purchase of Soviet arms equipment.

The Economic Aspect of Finnish-Soviet Relations

Moscow has monitored Finland's economic cooperation with Western institutions with prudent suspicion, departing from the premise that economic ties easily evolve into political ones. Finnish refusal in 1947 to join the Marshall plan was based on a correct understanding that a decision to do so would have caused a crisis in relations with Moscow. It was not until well after the thaw in 1955 that trade agreements could be reached with the OEEC countries and membership in that organization considered. Finland joined the organization, by then renamed the OECD, ten years later. When EFTA was created in 1959, Moscow immediately criticized this free-trade association of non-EEC Western European states, implying that it would be dominated by the U.K., would discriminate against the socialist states, and would thus be incompatible with neutrality. The neutral members, Sweden in particular, simply rejected the Soviet accusations, arguing that only trade matters were concerned and that all non-members were treated equally. Finland, which wanted a free-trade agreement with EFTA, had to act with more circumspection. It needed to persuade Moscow that an affiliation with EFTA would not mean political change, but that Finland had to protect its competitive standing in the West and that it would act in a way that would not jeopardize Soviet exports. A special agreement was finally concluded between Finland and EFTA, which testified both to Soviet willingness to take due account of Finnish economic interests in the West, and to the EFTA countries' understanding of Finland's wish to maintain her position in the Soviet market. Moscow's decision to agree was clearly made at the top, by Khrushchev, against some considerable opposition in the bureaucracy.

At the end of the 1960s, new problems surfaced for Finland when the EFTA members, headed by the U.K., began discussing membership in or other arrangements with the EEC. A Nordic cooperative scheme, NORDEK, was proposed, which was intended as a customs union in the area, but was also seen as an added trump card in later negotiations with the EEC. Moscow was suspicious and argued that NORDEK would lead to the integration of its members into the European Communities, which was then viewed, not only by the Soviets, as a dynamic and expansive organization. Helsinki decided in the end not to participate in the institutional preparations but to implement the trade measures contained in the NORDEK proposal. Finland's decision aborted the NORDEK plans, and Denmark proceeded to apply for EEC membership. Finland negotiated a free-trade agreement with the EEC, similar in practice to the Swedish one.

Concurrently, Finland made efforts to expand trade with the Soviet Union, which had fallen to only about 12 percent of total foreign trade. An agreement was concluded in 1973 on cooperation with the CMEA. In retrospect, Moscow might have been better served if it had accepted NORDEK, given the green light to Finland, and thus conceivably kept Denmark out of the Western European economic bloc. Once again, however, worst-case scenarios dominated Soviet thinking and exacerbated the Soviets' historical fear of Finnish integration in a Nordic community.

The Soviet Union is Finland's largest trading partner and accounts for almost one-quarter of Finland's foreign trade, followed by Sweden. Finland is the U.S.S.R.'s second-largest capitalist trading partner after West Germany. Total trade for the five-year period 1980-85 amounts to 25 billion rubles. Finnish-Soviet trade expanded greatly in the 1970s, after having stagnated since the mid-1950s. This expansion was due principally to the rapid increase in prices of oil, which accounts for 85 percent of Soviet sales to Finland. The Finnish economy has thus been able to overcome the oil price shock by expanding its exports of manufactured goods to the U.S.S.R. This extensive access to the Soviet market accelerated Finnish GNP growth and countered the negative effects of Western economic stagnation in the 1970s.

The future, however, might be gloomier. Lower energy prices and reduced oil consumption will decrease the volume of trade if it is not kept up for political reasons. Political considerations might make Finnish policy makers somewhat less eager to save gas and oil or entice them to promote investment in heavy industry, which uses a great deal of energy. Politics aside, easy access to the Soviet market for ships, textiles, etc., might preserve an industrial structure in Finland which is outdated in the advanced capitalist world. These aspects of the Finnish-Soviet economic relationship have been pointed out by critics, but the advantages get more publicity. In the future, the U.S.S.R. is likely to return to a more "normal" 15 percent to 20 percent share of Finland's foreign trade and structural problems will decrease in importance. Finland's long-term headache is likely to be how to prevent this share from falling even lower.

A NORDIC NUCLEAR-FREE ZONE

An issue of long-standing importance in Soviet-Finnish relations, as well as in Soviet-Scandinavian relations, has been the establishment of a Nordic nuclear-free zone. The idea was first mentioned by Bulganin in 1957. Two years later, Khrushchev expanded the proposal to cover "the Scandinavian peninsula and the Baltic area" at the same time that he also proposed a number of other nuclear-free zones to cover the Balkans, the Adriatic, Central Europe, and the Far East. These areas would be "parts of a broad zone of peace which could separate the armed forces of NATO and the Warsaw Pact." As to the zone in Northern Europe, it was declared that the U.S.S.R., together with the Western powers, would agree "to regard these countries as being out of bounds for rockets and atomic weapons and to respect the status quo in the area." This dual obligation, which has not been repeated in Soviet statements of recent years, would be enshrined in an agreement among the Baltic states, the states of Northern Europe, and the great powers.

The late 1950s saw proposals from both East and West to demilitarize Europe. In 1955, both Eden and Molotov proposed limits on troop levels and armaments in Central Europe, and advocated a demilitarized zone between East and West. The two proposals differed in that Moscow assumed a divided Germany with nuclear weapons prohibited in both parts of that nation. The British Labour party leader Gaitskell wanted foreign troops withdrawn from both Germanies (plus Poland, Czechoslovakia, and Hungary). American scholar-diplomat George Kennan proposed a simliar troop disengagement to be followed by the reunification and neutralization of Germany, and also proposed a ban on nuclear weapons in continental Europe. Polish Foreign Minister Rapacki suggested a prohibition on nuclear weapons, and on rockets for their delivery, in Poland, Czechoslovakia, and the two Germanies. The Nordic zone idea was thus part of a fairly lively East-West discussion.

The discussions in NATO on a multilateral nuclear force (MLF) fueled the debate in the early 1960s. The Russians linked this question to the Baltic region. In a note to Bonn on 8 April 1963, Moscow expressed its concern not only that West Germany might acquire nuclear weapons, but also that the Baltic might become a base area for the MLF fleet or for American submarines armed with nuclear weapons. Shortly thereafter, the U.S.S.R. proposed to all the littoral states of the Mediterranean that this sea become free of nuclear weapons.

Nordic interest in the idea was demonstrated by the proposal made in 1961 by Swedish Foreign Minister Unden aimed at creating nuclear-free zones in all of Europe. Later, in 1963, a specific proposal for a Nordic nuclear-free zone was formulated by Kekkonen. That proposal first received a cool reception in other Nordic capitals, but recently different versions of it have been discussed in more positive terms, principally by the governments of Finland and Sweden and by labor parties throughout Scandinavia. The main reasons behind the revival of interest in this issue have been the "new" nuclear debate in Europe, Soviet offers to include part of its own territory in such an arrangement, and a change of heart in the Norwegian and the Danish Labor parties. The issue is of more direct concern to Denmark and Norway since they would have to change their policies of maintaining a nuclear option in wartime. This contrasts with policies in Finland, whose non-nuclear status was established in the 1947 peace treaty, and Sweden, which decided in the early 1960s not to acquire nuclear weapons. All of the Nordic countries have ratified the Non-Proliferation Treaty. Although the deployment of nuclear weapons is not prohibited by this treaty, it is for all practical purposes ruled out in the cases of Finland and Sweden.

Moscow has supported the idea of a Nordic nuclear-free zone since it was first proposed, and has stepped up its efforts in recent years. However, it has been vague concerning problems, much discussed in the Nordic countries, associated with the establishment of such a zone, such as format, scope, geographic extension, links to continental Europe, etc. Bulganin's letters to Copenhagen and Oslo in 1957 no doubt reflected a genuine Soviet concern that Denmark and Norway would permit nuclear weapons to be installed on their territories. Such weapons could threaten targets in the Soviet Union or in other Eastern bloc countries, or, if they were only short-range weapons, be of considerable military importance in a conflict. That danger has receded, both because of the Soviet buildup of nuclear forces that act as deterrents and because Danish and Norwegian policies in peacetime have proved to be prudent, non-provocative, and, for all practical purposes, non-nuclear. Indeed, the nuclear weapons in Northern Europe belong almost exclusively to the Soviet Union.

Even though only a small fraction of the approximately 3,000 Soviet nuclear weapons that are deployed close to the proposed Nordic zone might now be intended for use against the Nordic area, many more are *capable* of reaching Nordic targets.

Norway and Denmark have both adopted policies of not admitting nuclear weapons in "peacetime." Because they lack both the expertise and the equipment that would allow their own military forces to use such weapons, the non-nuclear commitment, as far as their own forces are concerned, has become well-nigh unconditional. NATO forces, however, presumably would be able, if it were a sound idea militarily and if Norway and Denmark so permitted, to use their territories for nuclear missions.

Soviet interest in a binding, legal commitment on the part of Norway and Denmark can now be assumed to be more political than strictly military. The idea of an arrangement limited to Sweden and Finland, which has been proposed in the Nordic discussions, would be of only tactical interest to Moscow as a preliminary to the wider scheme. Iceland is a special case, but it is obviously in the Soviet interest to include this country in a non-nuclear zone.

A Nordic nuclear-free zone, according to Moscow, "could have a favorable effect on the international political climate and facilitate detente." It would foreclose the nuclear option for the two Nordic NATO states, even if they were highly provoked, which might give Moscow somewhat greater leeway in the region if it needed it. It would weaken the link between these countries and NATO, a long-standing Soviet priority which has even, at times, provoked Soviet commentators to talk wistfully of a Scandinavian military community. It could, if guarantees are given by the nuclear powers, provide the U.S.S.R. with a certain *droit de regard* with respect to Norwegian and Danish policies, since such an arrangement would have to be "effectively controlled." And it would, above all, give political support to the anti-nuclear forces in Western Europe, particularly in West Germany.

Nor are the military implications of a Nordic nuclear-free zone negligible from the Soviet perspective. In Moscow's view, the non-nuclear commitment of members of a Nordic zone would have to be "total," which could mean that a Soviet guarantee not to use nuclear weapons against the Nordic countries would not be given until certain issues, labeled by Soviet media as violations of already-existing Norwegian and Danish non-nuclear commitments, have been resolved. These issues include the preparation of bases to receive aircraft and submarines carrying nuclear weapons; the pre-stocking of artillery capable of firing nuclear munitions; facilities for AWACS aircraft "capable of directing nuclear bombers to their targets"; visits of vessels equipped with nuclear weapons to Norwegian harbors; and Loran-Omega radio navigation stations serving American nuclear-armed submarines in the North Atlantic. The U.S.S.R. stated, at the signing of the 1967 Tlatelolco treaty prohibiting nuclear weapons in Latin America, that "Any actions by a signatory that are incompatible with its non-nuclear status would make the Soviet Union reconsider its obligation." The same would no doubt apply to a Nordic zone.

For its part, the Soviet Union would promise not to use nuclear weapons against the Nordic region. Such assurances have already been given to Finland and Sweden in their capacity as non-nuclear-weapon states. In most conceivable military scenarios, the advantages of nuclear attacks against Norway and Denmark as compared to conventional attacks seem slight. As to whether solemn promises would be kept in wartime, doubts would in principle exist on both sides, since the Norwegians and the Danes could cheat as well as the Russians by allowing NATO nuclear forces into their territories.

The Soviets originally rejected the idea of nuclear restrictions on Soviet territory as a counterpart to a Nordic nuclear-free zone. That stand was explained as follows: "The position of the Soviet Union is entirely clear. The U.S.S.R. departs from the principle that the frontlines of a nuclear-weapon-free zone shall be decided in strict accordance with the accepted rules of international law, including free passage on the open seas and in those straits that are used in international maritime traffic. This means that the frontiers of the zone cannot be extended further than the borders of the participating states, including their airspace and their territorial waters. Furthermore, it must be noted that the Soviet Union is a nuclear power and that consequently neither its territory nor any part thereof can be included in a zone free from nuclear weapons or in a so-called security zone which is linked to the nuclear-free zone. The status of a nuclear-free zone must not prevent Soviet naval vessels from passing through the Baltic Straits with whatever weapons on board" (Y. Kommissarov in *Mirovaya ekonomika i mezhdunarodnye otnoshenija* (1979), p. 113). However, in reference to the Mediterranean, Moscow had already demonstrated that it could accept limitations on the deployment of nuclear weapons on board Soviet vessels. As Soviet interest in a Nordic nuclear-free zone grew, its position became more flexible.

This evolution was one of the main reasons why the issue acquired new life in Nordic political debate in the early 1980s. Brezhnev promised in 1981 "to examine the question of certain other measures applicable to our own territory in the areas adjoining the nuclear-free zone in Northern Europe." He added that such measures would be "substantial" (*Der Spiegel*, November 1981). Later, Andropov said that "the Soviet Union could also discuss with interested parties the question of giving nuclear-free status to the Baltic Sea" (*Pravda*, 7 June 1983). This was an interesting new development, for in recent times Khrushchev's ideas in the same direction had disappeared from public Soviet delarations. The Russians had instead often stressed the freedom of the riparian states to have whatever naval armaments they required in this area, especially since the U.S.S.R. had to move its vessels between the different seas.

The idea of including the Baltic in a Nordic nuclear-free zone must have been a controversial one within the Soviet Union. In a widely distributed book, *Non-Nuclear Status to Northern Europe* (October 1984), Lev Voronkov, a department head at the Institute for World Economy and International Relations (IMEMO) and a prolific writer on Nordic affairs, provides a detailed analysis of the security problems in the region and focuses on the "substantial Soviet measures" envisaged in Brezhnev's and Andropov's statements. These measures, Voronkov says, "depend on which countries will join the zone and under what conditions, whether guarantees will come from the Soviet Union alone or from the West as well, what sort of guarantees will be made by the West and on what conditions." Such questions can only be resolved through negotiations. On the Baltic, however, Voronkov is more explicit in commenting on the Swedish position that nuclear weapons in this region should be part of an arrangement:

> The Baltic Sea does not belong to the Soviet Union or to Sweden. Therefore, the Baltic problems cannot but concern all the littoral states here. Up to now, there is no arrangement to involve all the Baltic states, including Poland and East and West Germany, in discussions on the subject.
>
> This is probably not accidental. The Baltic Sea borders directly on Sweden as well as on Central Europe. To view this sea from the angle of the security problems of the Scandinavian subregion is groundless, and this can hardly be appreciated by the other Baltic states. The reason is simple: The importance of the Baltic by far exceeds the limits of the subregional problems.
>
> One should never forget that the Baltic Sea and the forces operating there constitute part of the European military balance. To overlook this is downright irresponsible. It would be wrong to deal with the Baltic problems exclusively from the viewpoint of a Northern European nuclear-free zone. . . . Why indeed is only the Baltic included in a nuclear-free zone and not the other seas washing the Scandinavian countries?

The best way to proceed, Voronkov suggests, would be to instead treat the Baltic as an important, separate issue among other initiatives to create nuclear-free zones in Europe (in the Balkan area, in the Mediterranean, a corridor in Central Europe, etc.) and not as a part of a Nordic zone.

Different opinions obviously exist in Moscow on this matter. Voronkov was soon contradicted by responsible party and government officials, but he could not have expressed himself with such candor without support from higher up. A certain vagueness on this score would seem to be in Soviet interests.

Perhaps a hundred tactical nuclear weapons are aboard Soviet ships in the Baltic, and many more are stationed on ships passing in and out. Medium-range ballistic missiles are part of the equipment of six Golf submarines which were introduced as late as 1977. In 1982, some additional MRBMs on Juliet-class submarines were reported. Presumably, there are no nuclear weapons on the ships of other riparian nations and there are no reports of any Western interest to introduce such arms in this area.

The Soviets have made other statements of interest in regard to a nuclear-free zone in the Nordic area in their frequent references to the problem of sea-launched or air-launched cruise missiles which would pass over Swedish and Finnish territory. It has been argued that an agreement on a zone would imply that the nuclear powers promise not to fire such weapons across the Nordic area. Moscow has not rejected the Nordic proposal that tactical nuclear weapons now stationed in the western part of the Kola Peninsula be included in an agreement. This would be the effect of the Palme Commission proposal to establish a corridor through the whole of Europe, 300 kilometers wide, free of tactical nuclear weapons.

Moscow has argued that the Nordic countries would first have to agree among themselves on a Nordic zone and then turn to the nuclear powers to negotiate the "guarantees." Such guarantees could be given unilaterally by the U.S.S.R. through a general agreement or through bilateral agreements with each of the Nordic countries, regardless of whether other nuclear powers agree to do the same. The negotiations would resolve the question of restrictions on Soviet nuclear weapons, and would presumably also specify in more detail the non-nuclear status of the Nordic countries.

SWEDEN

Soviet relations with Sweden throughout the late 1960s and the 1970s were uniformly good and "stable," a description coined by Brezhnev in his "Report to the Central Committee" in 1971. Swedish-Soviet relations were thus given little high-level attention in Moscow.

The issue of Swedish relations with the EEC, which had loomed as a potential source of friction between the two countries in the early 1960s, had disappeared. The Soviet view at the time was that membership in or association with the EEC would be incompatible with Swedish neutrality. The basic argument was that "a small country becomes so bound to its larger partners through institutionalized economic cooperation that its sovereignty is jeopardized"--it cannot avoid further commitments of a political-military nature. A small country in this position therefore runs the risk of having to assist NATO, limiting its freedom to trade and thus discriminating against the socialist countries, or becoming so implicated in the economic mechanism of the West that political options are closed. The Swedish government decided on its own to reject full membership in the EEC and opt for a wide-ranging free-trade agreement. This decision evoked satisfaction mixed with only vague criticism from Moscow.

Soviet criticism of the strength of the Swedish military, a perennial source of conflict, did not prevent increasingly cordial relations between the armed forces of the two countries during most of this period. An exchange of military visits took place in 1967, including a visit to Sweden by a group of Soviet MIG-21 fighters, the first time a Soviet military air unit had flown to a Western country. This was followed by several exchange calls of naval vessels to Leningrad and Stockholm, which were crowned by a visit to Sweden by the head of the Soviet Navy, Admiral Gorshkov. The Soviet invasion of Czechoslovakia interrupted these contacts, but visits took place between Soviet and Swedish defense ministers in the 1970s.

During this time, the international political context had changed as the Vietnam War absorbed the interest of both the political elite and the public in Sweden, leading to sharp criticism of U.S. policy and tension between Stockholm and Washington. The Soviet Union obviously praised this Swedish criticism, but Moscow was by no means spared by "the active neutral policy" that Sweden now pursued. The Swedish government, more strongly and persistently than most, attacked the invasion of Czechoslovakia and consequently reduced its contacts with the Russians. Moscow, apparently satisfied that the operation had been relatively painless in real international terms, suffered the Swedish criticism in relative silence.

Under the circumstances, Swedish criticism of the invasion of Czechoslovakia was no doubt expected and taken for granted. Moscow was probably more irritated when in the mid-1970s, with detente in full bloom, Sweden's Prime Minister Palme began to refer in his speeches on international affairs to three themes which touched raw nerves in Moscow: the danger of "superpower collusion" which overrode the interests of other states; the drawbacks of Communist ideology when put into practice; and the desirability of democratic socialism as an alternative to communism. The first of these themes, more unusual to hear from Sweden than the other two, particularly irked the Russians, not least because they had to contend with its positive echo in the Third World, where Palme enjoyed high standing.

Moscow's desire to minimize friction with Sweden was clear, however, and only indirect criticism was published. Likewise, two fairly obvious targets of Soviet criticism were treated discreetly. One was Sweden's efforts to sell its Viggen aircraft to four NATO countries with Swedish government guarantees that spare parts would be delivered even in wartime. Another was the Swedish decision to participate (with a neutrality proviso) in the Western energy organization IEA, then under heavy attack from Moscow.

Praise was heaped upon Sweden and its policies in the Swedish version of an official biography of Leonid Brezhnev, published in 1978 in conjunction with a visit to the U.S.S.R. by the Swedish royal couple. Neither the preface, which was signed by Brezhnev himself, nor the text, which quoted extensively from statements by the Soviet leader, contained a single discordant note to break the harmony which was said to exist between the two countries. "We in the Soviet Union attach great value to Sweden's neutral policy, which is one of the important factors contributing to peace and security in Northern Europe, and which also plays a positive role on the international scene," Brezhnev said, adding that this factor was growing in importance in international life. Sweden's active policies on international questions received exceptionally high praise, particularly in the field of disarmament. The Soviet leader said that the U.S.S.R. placed high hopes "on expansion of our cooperation with Sweden as well as with other peace-loving states in the continued work to achieve sound international relations."

Soviet media supported "workers' parties" in the 1976 elections. Indeed, the former arch-foe, "social democracy," had long been lauded for its "anti-imperialist attitude" on international questions, particularly in the Northern European countries. However, for the first time in the postwar era, Social Democratic power in Sweden was broken. The U.S.S.R. had no difficulties cooperating with the new bourgeois government.

The unanimous support in Sweden for its policy of neutrality was reflected in the lack of any sustained Soviet criticism of Sweden. The only cloud on the security horizon came not from Sweden but Norway, where NATO's "militaristic projects directly threaten the Swedes' and the Finns' security," according to a 1979 *Pravda* article. On 22 November 1980, the same paper said that those projects "cannot fail to reflect on the development of interstate relations in that region."

It was assumed by most Nordic commentators that Moscow, from both a "civilian" political viewpoint and a purely military perspective, saw the advantage of neutral Sweden as a big block of well-guarded territory, longer than the total land frontiers between the two power blocs south of the Baltic, which limited the deployment possibilities of both an aggressor and the attacked party and contributed to the military balance in the area. "Routine" Soviet criticism of Swedish defense efforts as too large for such a small country, too one-sided for a neutral nation, and too dependent on American technology, was written off, partly because it occurred only rarely. The voices heard from Moscow complaining about stepped-up NATO activities in Norway and Denmark were regarded as exaggerated, and in any case not directly related to Sweden. Nor was any great attention paid to new themes in military discussions in the East and the West. One of these themes was the increased emphasis being given to conventional warfare once parity had been established on the different rungs of the nuclear escalation ladder. Another was the tendency of modern warfare to combine theaters of armed operations and reduce geographical distances, thus bringing both Central Europe and the far North closer to central Scandinavia.

The Submarine Incidents

These fairly calm and untroubled waters were disturbed by a succession of submarine incidents beginning in 1980 along Sweden's Baltic coastline. The most important of these incidents were officially attributed to the Soviets. Submarines had been sighted before in both Swedish and Norwegian waters, but in these recent cases, the submarines had become much more visible, and one was actually caught. Moscow claimed that the submarines either did not exist or, in the one incontrovertible case, had gone astray.

There was some logic to the Soviet protestations that sending submarines into Scandinavian waters would be against their own political interests. This argument was made not only in the Swedish case but also in reference to rumors about Soviet submarines in Norwegian waters:

A well-rehearsed and preplanned anti-Soviet per-
formance. Its purpose is to create tension in the
countries of Northern Europe and cast suspicion
on the peace-loving Soviet policy . . . [and] to
provide a reason for whipping up anti-Soviet
hysteria, which plays right into the hands of
NATO strategy. (*Izvestija*, 7 May 1983.)

A similar set of accusations was made in the case of alleged
Soviet submarines in Swedish waters:

Swedish military circles and right-wing forces
want to use these submarine rumors to secure
new large appropriations for military purposes
and to push this neutral country toward the
aggressive NATO block . . . to weaken the
anti-war movement . . . and to sow seeds of
suspicion and hostility toward Eastern neighbors
and . . . undermine the traditional normal
relations between the U.S.S.R. and the Scandinavian countries. (*Pravda*, 12 October 1982.)

Such anti-Soviet exploitation of foreign submarines indeed
ran counter to Moscow's interests. *Pravda*'s description would
be apposite were there an internal Soviet debate on the matter
with some arguing against the advisability of letting military
considerations override political ones. Indeed, the analysis as to
the effects on Swedish and Nordic opinion was entirely correct.

The facts were as follows: Submarines had been sighted
occasionally throughout the late 1960s and 1970s, but they never
penetrated deeply into Swedish waters, and they always left
immediately after detection and warning by anti-submarine
forces. Beginning in 1980, however, the nature and pattern of
violations changed. Foreign submarines began to be discovered
close to sensitive military installations, and they conducted
evasive action when they were discovered. In 1981, a Soviet
Whiskey-class submarine ran aground outside Karlskrona, a
naval base in southern Sweden.

The salient features of this incident, in terms of Soviet
behavior, were that the submarine was sent deep into Swedish
territorial waters through an archipelago which is highly

complex to navigate, that it ran aground close to a Swedish naval base, and that it contained atomic weapons, anathema to the Nordic public and of no possible use for the mission assigned to it. It was difficult to dispel the impression of routine reconnaissance gone awry by a foolishly imprudent commander--a sinister prospect for the Swedes.

In their diplomatic negotiations with Sweden for the release of the vessel, the Russians placed a Soviet naval group in the area outside Swedish territorial waters, expressed regret over the "accident," and urged the Swedes to let matters rest there. While the submarine was in Swedish hands, Moscow--pained, no doubt, by international media attention to the sorry spectacle of its stranded submarine--allowed the Swedes, based "on the nature of Soviet-Swedish relations and by way of exception," to inspect the ship's documents and to interrogate crew members, but refused to allow them to search the interior of the vessel. After nine days, the submarine was "finally" released and the Soviet government, in a public declaration (*Pravda*, 12 November), "resolutely rejected" the Swedish protests and said that Sweden was "distorting the facts" by alleging that the submarine had entered Swedish territorial waters deliberately for "unlawful activities." The Soviet statement was couched in fairly subdued language and expressed a desire for continued "mutual respect, good-neighborliness, and cooperation" in relations with Sweden. A skeptic could have found a potential excuse for future violations in the statement that "emergency situations" are bound to happen at sea. It was also noteworthy in terms of future events that the Soviet declaration stressed that, according to international law, "if a foreign warship does not observe the rules of a coastal state regarding passage through its territorial waters, the only thing the coastal state may do with respect to the warship in question is to demand that it leave that state's territorial waters." (Compare this to the opposite analysis applied to the Catalina and Pueblo cases.)

A month after the Whiskey incident, a Moscow correspondent for the largest Swedish newspaper was de facto expelled for "attempting to gather information on defense matters, photograph military equipment and closed facilities," but no further sanctions, if that in fact was one, were imposed by Moscow.

In September/October 1982, a group of submarines was detected in Harsfjarden, a major naval base area in the archipelago near Stockholm. The sighting came after a series of reports of other suspected submarines in the area. An investigation of "track marks" on the ocean bottom indicated that miniature submarines had apparently been launched from conventional submarines. The search for the vessels themselves was unsuccessful, but a government commission later established, on the basis of signal intelligence, sonar contacts, "footprints," and other evidence, that the vessels belonged to the Soviet Union. The Swedish government lodged a strong protest.

In its reply, the Soviet government stated that the Swedish note was "an unfriendly act toward the U.S.S.R.," and claimed that no Soviet submarines had been closer than thirty kilometers from Swedish territorial limits at the time in question; that no reconnaissance was necessary since Sweden's excellent sea charts were available to the public; that the Soviet Union always respected international law and recognized borders; and that certain persons in the administration in Sweden had spread these fabrications, upon which the Swedish government had based its unfounded assertions which represented a campaign against the Soviet Union's peaceful policy.

> The Soviet government categorically rejects the Swedish government's protest as unfounded, and expects the Swedish government to carry out a new, objective investigation into the case, and to take to task those persons who have given it false material and conclusions.

The note ended with a statement of the desire of the U.S.S.R. for good neighborly relations with Sweden. Somewhat later, Moscow proposed that a joint Soviet-Swedish commission study the evidence. The Swedes rejected the proposal.

Various other incidents have since taken place in which the military has established the presence of foreign submarines, operating somewhat more prudently than earlier ones, in Swedish waters. However, it has been impossible to identify with certainty the nationality of these vessels. Consequently, no new official protests have been made, but, given the background, Swedish-Soviet relations have continued to be somewhat strained. Relations were not helped when the Soviets, true to their well-established practice, denied in autumn 1984 a flagrant intrusion of military aircraft over Swedish territory.

The Political Context

There have been a number of theories put forward to explain the Soviet submarine incursions, but few hold up under close examination. One hypothesis is that the Russians wanted to put political pressure on Sweden; this hypothesis has several variations. Military provocations, according to one version, would increase anxiety in Sweden and thus swing Swedish public opinion in favor of adopting a more amical posture--a "Finnish policy"--toward the Soviet Union. But to proceed in such manner to gain a political advantage would be a radical departure from traditional Soviet behavior toward Sweden; it would also make no sense, since the effect of such actions, predictably, goes against the Soviet interest, as was very succinctly stated by *Pravda.* If Moscow wanted to change Swedish policies, it would express dissatisfaction before embarking upon a highly visible pressure campaign. Soviet media, however, had not criticized Swedish foreign and defense policies before the incidents (except incidentally), and for some time afterward they dealt only with issues directly related to Swedish accusations and condemnations (discussed below). Indeed, Swedish viewpoints on issues where Stockholm's views might matter to Moscow, such as disarmament problems in the North and in Europe, were covered widely in the early 1980s as being unusually parallel to Soviet positions.

Another argument is that intrusions which cannot be prevented by the coastal state might weaken defense morale.

Once again, however, the incidents have had the opposite effect--more money is now being devoted to defense and the buildup of anti-submarine capacity seems to have forced the intruders to behave more cautiously. The Russians, who are traditionally suspicious of the permanence of Swedish neutrality, cannot but regret that recent polls have shown that 80 percent of the Swedish population now believe that the Soviet Union "has an unfriendly or a hostile attitude to Sweden," a direct result of the submarine affairs.

Other explanations, such as "reminding the Swedes of the U.S.S.R.'s superpower status" or "rubbing in the Soviet domination of the Baltic," underestimate Soviet self-assurance. Massive self-confidence is a more likely character trait of Soviet admirals than excessive modesty. Arrogance born of power might also be a part of the mental make-up. In any case, Moscow has not in the past found it necessary to engage in muscle-flexing only to prove its obvious strength to the Nordics.

Links between the submarine incidents and the Norwegian situation, which after all was said to create dangers for the Swedes, have been hinted at in the Soviet media only very indirectly, and understandably so, given Soviet protestations of innocence regarding the incidents. In an important article, *Izvestija* commentator Bovin stated:

> the growth of overall tension in international affairs, and in particular the intensification of NATO's military activity in the North European region and in the Baltic basin, naturally force the Warsaw Pact to be concerned about its security. This increases . . . the probability of undesirable incidents. . . . Our command is doing everything to insure that there are no more of them. (28 March 1984.)

That statement was unusual because it seemed to imply that there had indeed been some submarines in Swedish waters (apart from the Whiskey case) and because it established an implicit link to Norway, which had not been done in previous articles on the submarine question. Naval forays into Swedish waters are clearly counterproductive in that regard, however, because they tend to stiffen Norway's stand in support of NATO. To try to scare the Norwegians in this roundabout way is hardly a strategem that would occur to the highly capable Scandinavian specialists within the Soviet party and government bureaucracy. They know from earlier experience that harassment tends to strengthen Norwegian national resolve rather than weaken it.

Action against one Nordic country in order to influence the policies of another has previously been undertaken only against Finland. There are no signs that Moscow is in the process of adopting a new policy in this regard or that crude tools such as submarine incursions would be used in that context. While no policy link can thus be detected, a military connection cannot be discounted in that increased Soviet concern over Norway could conceivably, as Bovin intimates, produce stepped-up Soviet military activity in the Baltic as well.

Would increased tension in Europe, as a result of the chill in superpower relations and the INF issue, heighten Soviet aggressive tendencies? From Moscow's perspective, tension, both worldwide and European, has been greater in earlier periods, such as in the 1950s and early 1960s, but this did not provoke military acts or threats against any Scandinavian country, even though that tension was more directly linked to Central Europe and the Baltic. Second, if Western INF deployment and President Reagan's policies increase the risks of war, Moscow argues that this particular process could lead to a *nuclear* war which might escalate to a global nuclear exchange. In such a scenario, the Swedish coastline would play no political or military role. Indeed, on those issues Sweden is seen by Moscow as playing a useful political role in the vanguard of the nuclear disarmament movement. Thus, there is little logic in such an explanation.

Would Soviet submarine activity in Swedish waters represent a signal to the rival superpower, the United States, that Soviet strength is preponderant in the Baltic Sea and that this region therefore should be regarded as a zone of exclusive Soviet interest? This is a farfetched hypothesis. The existing balance of military strength in the Baltic speaks much more clearly than would such a quaint and provocative "signal." Such "signalling" is clearly counterproductive because, if anything, it would call forth not acceptance, but Western countermeasures. The Americans, in any case, did not seem to get the "signal," because they greeted the news of the Soviet intrusions with great glee as another reason why all countries must stand up against the aggressive and mendacious Soviet empire.

Might not such Soviet military incursions represent a test of general Western reaction to a Soviet advance in the North? Would it not be at least of interest to Soviet policy makers to study the psychological attitudes toward such military moves in the area? This idea, while impossible to dismiss outright, presumes that Russians are gamblers or addicted to war-games of very doubtful utility, something which is not borne out by recent history.

Intrusions have been going on for many years, in both Swedish and Norwegian waters, without their timing being linked to any political event or to the general political atmosphere. In the absence of any additional signs in Moscow, it seems premature to attach any great *political* significance to the fact that the violations have increased in frequency and become more active and provocative. Foreign policy considerations, while not instrumental or even important in the original decision to send in submarines, must of course have entered into the process once a bilateral conflict had arisen over the intrusions. It is likely that the political aspect has been seen more as a cost to be paid for military gains than as a benefit to add to the list. Foreign policy considerations might have difficulty prevailing in such a military matter. The activity had been going on for a long time without any apparent problems. If the incursions into Sweden (and Norway) are part of a more general pattern (Scotland? South Korea? Japan?), to stop them in one place would create uncertainty in the overall planning for all operations. As long as the military can promise that no submarine will be caught, opposing opinions have limited weight.

During periods of international tension, the military generally gets a more attentive hearing by political decision makers. Tough talk at the top makes it difficult to deny lower levels their demand for military penetration or exercises. Security in a military sense gets the highest priority.

Military Aspects

Military considerations must indeed have prevailed. Submarine incidents have taken place in Swedish waters during the 1960s and 1970s, and the intruding nation or nations might simply have become used to the possibility of undertaking at least some operations in this area. Incidents from 1980 to 1984, however, were by character, size, and frequency something new. This also coincided in time with an increased frequency of submarine incursions reported in Norwegian waters.

The Swedish government commission established to examine the Harsfjarden events concluded that the incidents could not be explained simply as intelligence gathering but were elements of an operational pattern--preparations for military operations in Swedish waters in the event of war. The reasons given for this conclusion were the larger size of the operations and the fact that, while submarines had earlier shadowed Swedish naval maneuvers and equipment tests, they were now increasingly directed against permanent defense installations along the coast. The military purpose of this new type of operation would be preparation for the landing of sabotage groups and special units, as well as the clearance of the extensive mine fields that are an important part of Swedish coastal defense. This would be useful in case of surprise attacks or quick conventional strikes by an aggressor. The Swedish commission did not reach any conclusions as to why at this moment such preparations were being made. It referred, however, to the increasing importance of the area of Northern Europe which links the Baltic to the North Atlantic.

Western analysts, such as John Erickson and Michael MccGwire, have arrived at similar conclusions. They emphasize the increasing importance of the Nordic area as a whole, see it as a unified theater of military operations, and stress the Soviet interest in examining and preparing to use submarine bases, ports, and coastline installations in a drawn-out conventional war. Referring to the incursions in the waters off the southern coast of Sweden (only about one-fifth of reported incidents), they stress that in such a war Sweden's coastline could be useful to the Soviets in circumventing NATO defense in the Baltic. Furthermore, the Swedish archipelago is seen as a good training ground for warning systems, minisubs, etc. The increased emphasis in the debate in both the East and the West on the possibility of a protracted conventional war, as opposed to a conflict which would quickly escalate to the nuclear level, highlights such considerations. A brief description of Soviet military positions in the Baltic, based on the works of John Erickson and Erling Bjol, among others, is thus warranted.

In the late 1950s, the Soviet Baltic Fleet and its air arm was the most powerful of the four Soviet fleets, and larger by far than the NATO forces in that region. In the 1960s, the Soviet strategy of coastal and home-water defense was changed in favor of a strategy which concentrated on global naval operations. As a result, the Northern Fleet was strengthened and the Baltic Fleet was reduced, particularly in the number of submarines, which dwindled from 150 in the mid-1950s to only about forty in active service at the beginning of the 1980s. Reductions were also made in the number of large service ships. However, the Warsaw Pact naval forces still greatly outnumber NATO forces in this region by four or five to one, and a considerable buildup, especially of airborne units, helicopters, and amphibious craft, has been reported for the past few years. Repair facilities in Baltic ports are also important, accounting for more than 50 percent of Soviet repair capacity.

The Soviet surface fleet in the Baltic has twenty to thirty modern missile-equipped ships, a large number of small ships and older escort ships, and a very considerable air arm, which is also capable of long-range attack on surface targets, presumably not only in this region but also farther west against sea transport or carrier groups in the North Sea or the Atlantic. The fleet also has considerable amphibious capacity for landing operations, either across the Baltic or toward the approaches. Some analysts, such as Zakheim, claim that this is the primary function of the fleet and that amphibious capacity is being expanded, which hints at possible use against Denmark and/or Sweden.

There seems to be agreement among Western observers that, while the available forces are fully sufficient to protect the Warsaw Pact flank and in fact to predominate in this area, they are hardly large enough for simultaneous attacks on Denmark and Sweden. The Swedish coastline in particular, with the exception of its southernmost part, is made up of a rich archipelago which can be strewn with minefields and is difficult to penetrate. Until the late 1960s, the Swedish navy had several large surface ships capable of operating far out in the Baltic, but it has since been transformed into a coastal fleet of smaller vessels. An amphibious attack against Sweden would still have to cope with strong resistance put up by the Viggen strike aircraft combined with fast missile boats and strong coastal artillery units. A prominent feature in the Baltic has been large-scale Warsaw Pact naval exercises which do not seem to be necessarily related to the defense of this area. These operations have over the past twenty years extended more to the west, closer to Denmark. Soviet naval presence in Kattegatt and Skagerack has also caused concern in Denmark that the country could be placed behind the Warsaw Pact defense line. Overall, the recent trend in the Baltic seems to be toward reduced warning time and a larger Soviet offensive capability.

The Western presence in the Baltic consists of fairly large-scale exercises, mainly west of Bornholm, and of intensive daily intelligence gathering by reconnaissance aircraft taking advantage of the unique opportunity to peer electronically deep into the Soviet heartland. In recent years, NATO has also invested considerably in modern West German submarines and

Tornado attack aircraft to lessen somewhat the imbalance in strength.

The main task of the Soviet Baltic Fleet seems to be operations within the Baltic, since any attempt to penetrate through the straits into the North Sea would entail great risks and costs. The size and vulnerability of this fleet might induce Moscow to consider alternative ports in the Baltic to be used in wartime.

To fulfill its defensive tasks, the Soviet military in this region must prevent NATO from acquiring bases from which sustained operations can be carried out. If NATO controlled Swedish coastline territory, the Soviet defense of the Northern flank could be threatened. Sweden's policy of neutrality includes, however, very sizable armed forces to meet attacks from any quarter. Soviet military actions to destroy base facilities and early-warning systems or to occupy small parts of the coastline would perhaps be feasible, but they entail the risk of drawing in forces from the opposite side and thus creating the danger that was to be averted. Even if quick surprise actions succeeded on a few selected points, they would not serve the purpose of preventing NATO from controlling other Swedish territory. Furthermore, it is difficult to see how Swedish naval installations would greatly benefit Soviet operations in the Central European theater, since Soviet forces already command a large part of the Baltic coastline.

Instead, the submarines have been discovered in geographical locations that indicate an interest in possible penetration of the Swedish heartland. This contingency had not been among the priority scenarios in Swedish defense planning. The question is whether it has become more likely now. American generals do not usually underestimate Soviet military strength or ambitions, so an expert view from this quarter is of special interest. The scenarios envisioned by the Swedes in discussions of Soviet intentions with regard to the submarines is analyzed as follows by Major General (Ret.) Richard Bowman:

> The two remaining Soviet options for
> attacking the northern flank also involve wider

war. The first of these would be a Soviet effort to outflank the central front by moving into both Sweden and Norway. But as long as Swedish defense forces remain at current levels, choosing this option would mean adding at one stroke some 30 Swedish brigades and one of the strongest air forces in Europe to the side of the Alliance.

The Soviets would have to choose between risky amphibious operations across the Baltic, and a land campaign through northern Sweden and across the mountains into Norway. The Swedish air force and navy are prepared to move quickly to the threatened areas to blunt any attack until ground forces can take up defensive positions. Also, Sweden has well-trained local forces which stand ready to destroy roads and bridges, blocking every defile in northern Sweden. Soviet movement through southern Sweden, where most of Sweden's 30 brigades would be mobilized, would be even more difficult in terms of both Swedish defense and Soviet supply lines. To have any hope for success against the combination of Swedish, Norwegian, and Alliance reinforcement forces, the Soviets would have to commit at least 20 to 30 divisions and many tactical aircraft, which would certainly risk an early Alliance victory in the central region.

The final Soviet option on the northern flank would be to move against southern Norway via the Danish Straits. The Soviet capture of southern Norway, of course, would have an even greater effect on the sea war than the capture of northern Norway. Soviet naval and air forces operating from southern Norway could dispute passage throughout the North Sea and could threaten key bases in the United Kingdom. But southern Norway can be attacked only by first taking northern Norway, Sweden, or the Danish Straits. A major attack through the Danish Straits would be the most difficult and risky of the three approaches. As long as NATO is successful in its central region defense, any attack against the Danish Straits would be vulnerable to flanking attack from the Federal Republic of Germany on the south as well as Norway on the north. Nor would it be possible to move through

the Danish Straits by either sea or air in the face
of Allied mining and air forces based in
Germany, Denmark, Norway, and the United
Kingdom. Only the collapse of NATO's central
front would make invasion of Denmark and
southern Norway practical; if such collapse were
imminent, it would be prevented by the use of
nuclear weapons. (*Armed Forces Journal
International*, vol. 121, no. 9 (April 1984).)

Finally, whatever military benefits might have been gained
from the submarine operations in terms of reconnaissance
information or military preparedness, they will probably have
been offset by the obvious result of the incursions, which is that
the Swedes will have to increase defense spending precisely to
meet such contingencies, which hitherto have been given low
priority. The Swedish public, far from becoming accustomed to
and thereby tacitly accepting foreign incursions, has instead
demanded greater military capability to combat the intruders.
This is no easy matter as Sweden has 1,600 miles of coastline to
defend. To remedy deficiencies in anti-submarine warfare
capacity, $280 million will be spent by 1994. Generally,
military expenditures have been increased over planned amounts.
These increases have been criticized by Moscow, which views
Swedish defense as being directed essentially against the East.

Soviet Views on Swedish Neutrality

What does Moscow want out of Sweden in peacetime, over and
above what it already has? Soviet commentators sometimes
claim, as Voronkov did in 1984, that "neutrality" is less
important than Sweden's duty to make "peace efforts."
Concurrently, initiatives actually taken by recent Swedish
governments, mainly in the field of disarmament, are praised.
The Soviet Union, according to its media, wants a smaller
Swedish armed force. What bothers Moscow more than the
actual strength of Sweden's defense forces, which has decreased
in relative terms over the years, seems to be its structure and its

high technology, which creates links to, among other things, the American arms industry. This is nothing new, although perhaps the scope of such cooperation has increased slightly over the years. The Swedish defense industry, however, fulfills more than 75 percent of the country's need for arms and equipment, which comparatively is a very high percentage. Some advanced systems have to be acquired from the West, but whatever negative effects this might have on Russia's view of Sweden should be counterbalanced by a more solid and profound understanding in Swedish military circles of the value and demands of neutrality. The Swedes indeed argue that no neutral state relies so much on its own arms production as Sweden and is thus so impervious to pressure from outside contributors. No country produces all its defense material at home, but Sweden takes special care to avoid dangerous dependence on any one country in this field. As no one can suspect Stockholm of any aggressive ambitions, a great power which has no ulterior motives should support the idea of a strong Swedish defense. In particular the U.S.S.R. should appreciate the barrier that the Swedish air force represents against possible attacks across its territory on northwestern parts of the Soviet Union and the fact that a weakening of the Swedish air force might induce NATO to strengthen its air capability in Norway.

Moscow often expresses the wish to have more formalized cooperation with Sweden, such as regular consultations on foreign policy matters. The Russians would also like documents describing agreed principles that should guide relations between the two countries. Moscow would certainly appreciate the opportunities created by such procedures to influence Swedish positions, but it cannot now expect to have those long-standing wishes fulfilled.

Perhaps Moscow would like more extended economic cooperation with Sweden. Only 1 percent to 2 percent of Sweden's foreign trade is now with its giant neighbor. The Russians already have a large export surplus, mostly due to deliveries of energy and raw materials, and they have ample opportunity to increase their purchases in the Swedish market.

However, prospects for a large and steady exchange are not improved by Soviet hints that politics and trade go together. The American embargo on sales of high technology creates considerable problems for the Swedes. The prevalence of American components in Swedish advanced industrial products in effect prevents sales of a wide range of sophisticated equipment to the East. This of course is also true for other countries such as neutral Austria, which has a considerable trade with the U.S.S.R. and other COMECON countries.

What is the Soviet view of neutrality? What respect, if any, does a great power pay to the political choice of a small neighbor? Clearly, distinctions must be made between policies in peacetime, in crises, and in wartime.

In the 1920s and 1930s, the Soviet Union concluded a series of "treaties of non-aggression and neutrality" with bordering states (Afghanistan, China, Finland, Iran, Estonia, Latvia, Lithuania, Poland, and Turkey). The parties undertook to abstain in peacetime from participating in any military or political alliances or in any financial or commercial boycotts organized against the other party. The treaties did not deal with wartime situations, but only with how normal peaceful relations should be maintained, and they served Soviet interests well during a long period of weakness. When war broke out, however, the Soviets lost interest in the treaties, and the U.S.S.R. violated the stipulations of all of them. It remains part of Soviet foreign policy to appreciate the peacetime advantages of having neutral states in the capitalist world, but to retain its options on conceivable wartime situations.

It is impossible to say what considerations other than strictly military ones would guide Soviet policy makers--or, for that matter, the policy makers of any great power--in a European war. Whether any great power involved in a war will respect a small state's neutrality (that is, not attack Sweden, for instance) in wartime is a question that obviously can only be answered hypothetically. The answer depends on what kind of a war it is (nuclear or conventional; drawn-out or short; low-level or high-level fighting; worldwide, regional, or local), on what kinds of costs an attack would incur (how strong the Swedish defense would be; other demands on the forces of the attacker; the risks of riposte by other parties), on what kind of gains could be envisaged (military and/or economic), and on the whole political and military situation surrounding the conflict (who started it, and why). It would be foolish to try to give a general answer to such a multitude of questions covering specific and divergent hypothetical situations. Different scenarios, however, can be discussed, and their implications for Swedish security evaluated.

Military strategists in Moscow and elsewhere of course prepare for a variety of contingencies. Their plans do not necessarily indicate their real intentions, but rather are intended to lay out the possible military options they want to have available in any given theoretical situation. Policy makers, on their hand, must choose from among a range of options, military and otherwise, within the context of an actual situation. When all that has been said, it remains obviously ominous to a neutral state if it receives substantive information that plans are being made within great-power military staffs for attacks against its territory in a possible war situation.

When the Russians say that they respect Sweden's neutrality, they refer only to peacetime and crisis situations. They do not talk about wartime, because they do not know themselves what will happen then. When Denmark and Norway are told by the Soviets that participation in NATO will increase the risk that they will be involved in a future war, any *e contrario* conclusions regarding Soviet attitudes vis-a-vis neutral Sweden are obviously hazardous as Soviet propaganda on such an issue has low credibility. However, all concerned, including Moscow, would agree that neutrality serves as a protection in wartime only if the neutral state can persuade the belligerents that its territory will not be used by the enemy, which requires confidence both in its neutral policy and in its defense capacity. In both these regards, it is of course possible for the neutral state to have already fortified or weakened its credibility in peacetime.

If Soviet analysts could be persuaded to express themselves on the issue of Moscow's attitude toward neutral states in wartime, they might very well claim that in a major European war no country, neutral or not, could expect to be spared. This in itself would justify the Soviet demand for more active peace efforts on the part of the neutral, and it would also reflect the Russians' apocalyptic view of what a war in Europe would entail. It would not, however, necessarily reflect any high-level planning.

As argued above, the submarine intrusions into Swedish waters have principally to do with military contingency planning in the event of a European war. However, in terms of the peacetime situation, there is considerable evidence that Swedish neutrality is not only accepted in Moscow, but is perhaps viewed in a positive light. In any case, it is regarded as not amenable to any radical change.

The Soviet Media and Sweden in the 1980s

An analysis of the Soviet media treatment of Sweden and the other Nordic countries during the 1980s might throw some light on Soviet motives and thinking. Some preliminary comments on the reading of such political texts should be made, since an understanding of the purpose behind those critiques and attacks can be had only if the techniques employed in Soviet propaganda are understood.

One such technique is to make accusations not so much because the Soviet authorities believe them to be true, but because the accusations might call forth protestations of innocence from the accused party and assertions that whatever was in question will not happen. Norway has often experienced this "preemptive" technique. The object of Soviet criticism has been to receive continued assurances of Oslo's intention to maintain firm restrictions in its base and nuclear policies and make the Norwegians limit their options. Thus, Soviet positions are moved forward. It might be that Sweden is now being subjected to similar treatment.

A related tactic is to criticize aspects of a nation's policy, not because those aspects might be new, particularly objectionable, or less than "neutral," but simply as a way of exercising more or less gentle pressure and perhaps exploiting an auspicious political moment. If such media tactics fail or turn out to be counterproductive, they are discontinued--for the time being.

The Russians collect for future use. Sometimes brief pieces will appear in the Soviet press, often without commentary, quoting foreign media sources about something reprehensible, such as Swedish efforts to sell its Viggen aircraft to NATO countries. If general relations are good, the matter might be passed over altogether. The "books" are kept in good order, though, and the event is duly noted on the debit side, to be brought forward when bilateral relations or the regional or international situation give sufficient reason. Thus, silence does not mean approval.

On the other hand, criticism does not necessarily denote indignation over the specific matter under attack. In bad times, practically everything can be used. During the past several years, a series of Soviet accusations has been leveled at aspects of Swedish defense policy which are said to run counter to neutrality. The accusations were either untrue, or else they concerned old and well-established practices which the Soviets had not criticized publicly for a long time or at all. Two mechanisms had started working, however. The Karlskrona incident, in which the Russian military had been humiliated, called for a riposte, such as "revelations" to the public that the Swedes were also engaged in espionage. The Swedish media attacks on the U.S.S.R. and the official protests from Stockholm also necessitated a reply in kind. Thus, sharp criticism ensued, but this did not signal a new and politically more aggressive stand. A careful reading indicated instead a desire in Moscow to de-escalate the polemics and get back to normal business, at least with the friendly segment of Swedish political society.

Indeed, the Russians make careful distinctions. Media attacks are scrupulously targeted, ranging from "certain circles" outside the government to precisely identified individuals and officialdom to direct personal attacks on foreign heads of government and state. In Sweden, the right-wing opposition is sometimes named in media attacks, whereas the Social Democrats are normally spared.

The intensity and sharpness of the criticism obviously varies. Quoting from internal debates is a popular and fairly mild form of reprobation. The smallest local papers are read by assiduous Soviet officials in search of suitable quotations. At the other end of the spectrum are the solemn and sometimes threatening pronouncements issued in serious situations when patience is short. Sweden has not been subjected to such treatment; rather, disputes such as the submarine issue have been treated lightly. Submarine reports are met with satirical comments, although Soviet humor in this area tends to become somewhat heavy.

Thus, tactics decide what news should be published. Interference in other countries' internal affairs through media attacks on individual politicians alternate with total silence on important bilateral issues. Official Swedish protests and public commotion in September 1984, when a Soviet military aircraft clearly violated Swedish airspace, were given no publicity whatsoever. The protest, according to well-established practice, was rejected as unfounded. Shortly thereafter, the Soviet media published a report on a Swedish violation of Norwegian airspace, as if to show that the Swedes had made much ado about nothing.

Moscow carefully scrutinizes the internal political scene in democratic countries, and tries to steer its propaganda in channels most likely to lead to positive change. But detailed knowledge of political debates and conflicts does not necessarily imply a corresponding understanding of how people will react to criticism and propaganda. In recent years, Sweden and Norway have perhaps provided good examples on that score.

Soviet media attention to Sweden has been uncharacteristically intense during the past several years, reflecting the unusual tension between the two countries. The same is true for Norway, although, in contrast to Sweden, it is covered almost entirely in negative ways. Little attention has been devoted recently to Denmark. Finland is, as usual, given far more coverage than all the other Nordic countries, mainly regarding frequent high-level political visits and favorable Finnish political statements.

It should be noted that Norway had been under attack from the Soviet media with varying intensity since the late 1970s, while Sweden was normally given lavish praise until the submarine incident. Discordant notes appeared mainly with regard to NATO's bad behavior (a *Tass* report on 5 October 1979 accused West German combat planes and NATO vessels engaged in large naval exercises of "repeatedly violating neutral Sweden's frontiers"). Although the rule was that Sweden should be praised, there were sporadic complaints in early 1980 about the new Swedish JAS aircraft and Sweden's plans to equip it with imported American components, some criticism of excessive Swedish military budgets, etc. The apparent reason for the criticism was simply that the Russians disliked the JAS project, which was the single most important defense decision that the Swedes had made and would make for a long time. If the bilateral climate had been worse, much more acerbic comments would no doubt have been made. The theme was a familiar one, though, since decisions on earlier generations of combat aircraft had also been attacked. There is not a very great difference between the JAS and the earlier Viggen aircraft in terms of foreign technology. Both have American engines, and their air-to-air missiles are likewise American, although the JAS will have slightly more foreign electronic components than the Viggen. One would expect the Russians to prefer Swedish domestic production to purchase from abroad or to production under a NATO license. However, such reasoning was not shared in Moscow, which saw other alternatives for the Swedes, such as a radical cut in defense efforts.

Soviet media treatment of Sweden from 1981 through 1984 has consisted mainly of reaction to waves of anti-Soviet opinion in that country as a result of the various submarine incidents. Soviet articles have been primarily rebuttals of Swedish charges, and attacks on Swedish policies have seemed intended "to redress the balance" rather than to launch aggressive campaigns. Opportunities have been taken to publish positive Swedish statements when they were made, and distinctions among the different Swedish political groups have been carefully observed and calibrated according to the prevailing political situation. Seldom has the Swedish government itself been criticized, and then only mildly for having been misled. "Official circles" were sometimes taken to task, but most of the attacks were directed at "right-wing forces" and the military. Because most of the tension has been due to military matters, *Krasnaya Zvezda*, the army newspaper, is a frequent contributor to the debate in fairly polemical style. *Pravda*, which carries greater political weight, makes the most important conciliatory policy pronouncements.

The Whiskey incident in October 1981 provoked some scornful articles--after the submarine had been let loose--on the absurd Swedish allegations. No campaign was started, however, and the few critical articles devoted to Sweden in the months after the incident were still, by Soviet standards, fairly subdued. It was clear that Moscow did not want to unduly upset the Swedes and preferred to have the whole matter forgotten. Some items, however, had to be written as post-mortems or as warnings. Both Sweden and NATO were described as being actively engaged in electronic surveillance in the Baltic, and the Swedish defense budget was criticized as being excessively large (no doubt the result of the war scare created by the submarine). U.S. interference and the dependence of Swedish firms on American weapons technology, as in the JAS project, were said to cast doubt on Sweden's nonaligned status. These articles could be seen as preparing the readership for worse to come, but they probably only reflected the general coolness in relations that had come about because of the incident. Noteworthy was the increasing emphasis on the positive aspects of social democracy in Scandinavia, and on the negative features of the bourgeois, and particularly the Conservative, parties.

The first article about the submarine incidents which occurred in the summer of 1982 was published in *Krasnaya*

Zvezda on 5 August 1982. The article referred in fairly harsh terms to the "spreading [of] anti-Soviet lies not in keeping with Sweden's neutrality," but the blame was put on "certain circles" and the government was untouched. The submarine hunt in October went almost unnoticed in the Soviet media, with the exception of *Tass* reports about incidents "invented by military and right-wing circles to get higher military appropriations and draw Sweden closer to NATO." The neutrality declaration by the new Swedish government and by Prime Minister Palme himself were praised. On 21 November, *Krasnaya Zvezda* attacked aggressive Norwegian behavior and American machinations as indications that Scandinavia was being prepared as a bridgehead for aggression against the U.S.S.R. Sweden was mentioned in the article only with regard to NATO's attempt to implicate it in its war plans. On the whole, however, the Soviets attempted to soft-pedal the conflict through most of 1982.

An article in *Trud* on 20 January 1983 opened the new year with a re-examination of Sweden's previous bourgeois governments. These governments had not been criticized during their tenure (1976-1982); in fact, they had been officially praised along with some other governments for "their basically realistic approach to the solution of international problems and the positive tendencies in their foreign policy as regards detente, disarmament, and the extension of European cooperation" (*Soviet Foreign Policy, 1945-80*, A. A. Gromyko and others, eds., p. 592). Now, however, the interpretation of past events had changed: "Sweden's traditional neutrality shifted to the right over the past six years of bourgeois government. The threat of the country's gradual involvement in NATO's adventurist preparations had been growing increasingly real." Palme, the new prime minister, was described as steering a new course: a Nordic nuclear-free zone would be promoted, and policies for peace, detente, and disarmament would now be followed. At the same time, strong attacks were made against Norway's assiduous military buildup and against Norwegian Prime Minister Willoch, who was seen as the main agent for NATO.

The report of the Swedish submarine commission at the end
of April 1983, which incriminated the U.S.S.R. for sending
submarines deep into Swedish waters, provoked an exchange of
accusations and counter-accusations between Stockholm and
Moscow. The Soviet arguments were, of course, faithfully
recorded and repeated in the Soviet media. The targets of the
Soviet attacks were "certain persons in the state administration
and in politics," as well as the military, whose generals were
referred to as "liars from the Swedish Ministry of Defense." The
Soviet note sternly admonished the Swedish government to "take
to task those persons who had given it false material and
conclusions." This admonishment was recalled in a later report
on internal Swedish political conflicts, during which the prime
minister attacked the Conservative party (*Izvestija*, 3 June
1983). "Official Sweden" continued to be criticized as being too
close to NATO, but Prime Minister Palme was praised for his
comments on Reagan's nuclear policies (*Krasnaya Zvezda*, 4
June 1983), and for his active support of the Nordic nuclear-
free zone (*Izvestija*, 24 June 1983).

In September, *Krasnaya Zvezda* stepped up its attack on
"official Sweden and its cooperation with NATO." The theme of
the attack was "Swedish generals and Swedish neutrality are two
different things." Six items were focused on: Swedish officers
were regularly trained in the United States; NATO officers had
"inspected" Swedish military institutions, been trained in Swedish
aircraft simulators, flown the new Viggen airplane, etc., as if
"studying the future theater of war"; NATO weapons and
military equipment had been shipped through Sweden to
Norway; Swedish military maneuvers were sometimes held so as
to coincide with NATO exercises; modern military equipment
was purchased in large quantities from the U.S., and agreements
on the exchange of military information had been concluded
with Washington; and detailed maps of Sweden which could be
used for cruise missile planning had been given to the
Americans (*Krasnaya Zvezda*, 21 September 1983;
Komsomolskava Pravda, 4 January 1984). Swedish journalists
who interviewed party and military officials in Moscow at this

time reported a tough and critical attitude on the part of the soldiers (General Tatarnikov), who referred to the above "evidence"; stronger support for Swedish neutrality on the part of party officials (Zagladin); and skepticism (authorized?) of Swedish defense capabilities among institute researchers, who returned to an old Soviet theme--the uselessness of small states maintaining expensive military organizations.

Sweden's and Finland's defense capacity to prevent American use of Nordic territory or airspace for cruise missile or bomber attacks against the U.S.S.R. was brought up several times during this period. This issue was used principally in arguments for a nuclear-free zone which would entail guarantees from the nuclear powers not to violate Nordic airspace in such a manner. General Tatarnikov noted that the U.S.S.R. would not look on passively while such weapons followed their trajectories over Scandinavia (*Hufvudstadsbladet*, 11 December 1983). Actually shooting down such weapons, however, was said to be primarily the responsibility of the country concerned, and, in a positive vein for once, the Swedish military was reported to have invested resources in such a capacity (*Krasnaya Zvezda*, 12 February 1984). "Kommissarov" hinted at the link between cruise missiles over Finland and the FCMA treaty (15 January 1984), but others stressed the role of Finnish defense in such contingencies. Some articles, in describing NATO activities in Norway (such as airfields for U.S. nuclear bombers which might overfly Sweden and Finland on their way to the U.S.S.R.), stressed Oslo's inter-Nordic responsibilities. However, Swedish "anti-Soviet activities" were never treated as damaging to Soviet-Finnish relations in this tense period.

The negative treatment of Sweden in the Soviet media at the end of 1983 and the beginning of 1984 was by no means polemically extreme by Soviet standards. The Swedish government, and particularly its prime minister, was treated well when the opportunity arose; "periscope fever" was attributed mainly to the media and the military. American cruise missiles and violations of Swedish airspace were described as the real threats that the Swedes should worry about. The impression gained during this troublesome period in Soviet-West European relations was that the U.S.S.R. now felt the need for friends in neutral quarters (witness the splendid relations with another European neutral, Austria). The effect of other Nordic problems, particularly of Norwegian NATO activities and of increased U.S. interest in the Northern flank, clearly sharpened the conflict between the U.S.S.R. and Sweden, as was stated in an article by Bovin, whose main goal seemed to be to dampen the friction between Moscow and Stockholm (*Izvestija*, 28 March 1984). Those efforts were reinforced in March and April by several positive articles on Swedish policies. *Pravda*, on 15 March, lauded "Sweden's anti-militarist and anti-imperialist foreign policy" and "the Swedish leadership's constructive stand on international issues," dismissing "right-wing circles and NATO pressures" with the statement that "they do not determine Soviet-Swedish relations." Those "circles" could be identified by a sharp *Tass* attack on the leader of the Conservative party, in an attempt to exploit the political row going on in Sweden over the handling of Swedish-Soviet relations.

The stage was set for a new, more "normal" phase in the relationship. *Pravda*, on 15 April, even went so far as to link Sweden and Finland in criticizing U.S. Secretary of Defense Weinberger for trying to undermine "the peace-loving foreign policy of both these countries [Finland and Sweden] which advocate and support important initiatives in favor of detente and disarmament, and strive for broad cooperation with the U.S.S.R. and other socialist countries."

Ridicule of the submarine scare in Sweden also gave way to subtler talk. The Swedes were asked with increasing insistence whether these purported submarines did not in fact belong to NATO: "It is known that the U.S. has employed mini-submarines for reconnaissance. The Americans clearly have an interest in creating discord between the U.S.S.R. and its Scandinavian neighbors" (*Mezhdunarodnaya Zhisn*, June 1984). At the same time, the message was given to Stockholm, in a note from the Soviet government on the occasion of the 60th anniversary of diplomatic relations between the two countries, that Sweden should adopt more "realism" in its policies, a new and perhaps ominous recommendation.

The summer of 1984 was marked by continued irritation, increased by a clear Soviet violation of Swedish airspace and subsequent rejection of Stockholm's protest. Swedish journalists were granted extensive interviews in Moscow, because the Soviets assumed that critical comments on Swedish policies would get good coverage and therefore serve some useful purpose.

The official Soviet protestations of a continued desire for good relations were combined with an ambitious book-length analysis and critique of Nordic policies and Swedish neutrality which was published in the early autumn of 1984. In a new effort to improve relations, very few important articles on Sweden have been published since then.

DENMARK

The Soviets have paid little attention to Denmark during the period under review. Comments have been mostly positive and criticism has been muted in comparison with the treatment of the other Nordic NATO member, Norway. Public opinion in Denmark is hailed as effecting positive government stands on peace and disarmament issues.

In 1976, the Danish government agreed with Moscow to

> periodically hold consultations on international problems of mutual interest and bilateral questions. . . . Should situations arise that in the opinion of both sides create a threat to peace or a violation of peace or that cause international tension, both governments will contact each other to exchange opinions.

Regular consultations were agreed upon, and foreign ministers were scheduled to meet at least once a year (*Soviet-Danish Protocol on Consultations*, 6 October 1976).

Sweden for its part has had to be more circumspect because of its neutral status, and has long refused any agreement to conduct regular or automatic political consultations with the U.S.S.R. In practice, however, Sweden has attempted to maintain contacts at the highest level, which becomes more difficult in times of tension between the two countries. Norway has also refrained from agreeing to such consultations because it is wary of giving Moscow permanent and regular opportunities to apply pressure, but in practice it too has maintained a similar or even higher level of exchange to discuss bilateral problems. Finland engages in frequent exchanges at the highest level and its president and prime minister meet yearly with top Soviet leaders, a practice which, though not formalized, has become routine.

Tension in Europe in the 1980s has affected Danish-Soviet relations. Soviet media have reacted positively to the evolution of Danish public opinion on security matters. Moscow has taken every opportunity in the 1980s to participate in Scandinavian debates on defense and foreign affairs. In contrast to before, these public discussions have become frequent and increasingly sharp. The reasons are fairly obvious. They include the evolution of American strategy in favor of "extended deterrence" and a greater role for nuclear weapons in Europe, the INF issue and West German public debate, President Reagan's East-West and North-South policies, which are provocative to the Left everywhere, and the end of detente and the resulting need to invest more in defense during an economic recession. Added to those general, international factors are regional issues, which are sometimes difficult to interpret and evaluate. These regional issues include the Soviet submarine incursions in Scandinavian waters, the revival of the proposal for a Nordic nuclear-free zone, and the need born out of technical-military evolution to plan and prepare for faster Allied assistance in armed conflict. It is no wonder that bourgeois and social democrat parties came to diverge on which policies to pursue. Moscow thought it entirely appropriate to take a position on these disputes.

Throughout the 1970s, social democracy in the Scandinavian countries, once counted among the worst enemies of the Soviet state, was seen by the U.S.S.R. as a potential supporter of peace and progress. "Rightist social democrats" were on the defensive, and progressive forces were taking over. Nowhere was this as pronounced as in Denmark. A moderate response to the Afghanistan invasion, opposition to increased defense spending, a more radical stand against nuclear weapons in Denmark, more pronounced doubts on the INF project, and greater openness to the idea of a nuclear-free zone in Northern Europe were political positions that received praise in Moscow. They were deemed particularly important as they reflected not only a Danish or a Scandinavian stand, but social-democratic attitudes all over northwestern Europe, most forcefully advocated by the German SPD.

All was not rosy, however, between Moscow and Copenhagen, even when Social Democrats were in power. Danish and Norwegian participation in large-scale NATO maneuvers was criticized for being "in areas in immediate proximity to the U.S.S.R. in the North Atlantic and even in the Baltic Sea" (*Pravda*, 4 August 1981). *Krasnaya Zvezda*, in a major article in October 1981, examined "the provocative trend of the U.S. and NATO armed forces maneuvers" in the Baltic, and saw them as part of a general scheme to put pressure on the U.S.S.R. and influence the situation, primarily in Poland.

The Danes for their part have criticized the pattern of Soviet naval maneuvers, which until the early 1980s drew westward, taking place off the East German coastline and including amphibious assault exercises west of Rugen. For many years, other military activities involving Warsaw Pact forces have taken place regularly, including East German landing craft sailing around Zealand and Soviet bombers flying close to Danish airspace. In this regard, however, the situation has not changed in any ominous way in recent years.

Moscow has, as in the past, objected to the arrangement for the Allies to provide reinforcements and guarantees to Denmark, which is a fundamental aspect of Danish security policy. Danish defense rests on integrated Danish-West German forces within the joint command of BALTAP (under Danish command) and on external reinforcements in time of crisis. Agreements were signed in 1976 that Denmark would prepare four airfields to receive five U.S. Air Force squadrons in case of a crisis, under the Collocated Operating Bases (COB) program. Arrangements have also been made for U.S. and British troops (including two British air squadrons which have been added recently) to be assigned to BALTAP in such a contingency; some of these troops would be earmarked for Denmark and the rest for Schleswig-Holstein and Norway. These arrangements do not include base facilities, but they presumably do require that Denmark stockpile ammunition, spare parts, fuel, logistical supports, and so on. In contrast to Norway, no prepositioning agreements regarding heavy military equipment have been signed, because of Danish political reluctance and lack of U.S. initiatives. The arrangement does not represent much in terms of land reinforcement, but added to other defense policy decisions, such as cooperation in the unitary command, it is a step toward integrating Denmark further into the common NATO defense.

It is also important to note that Denmark for all practical purposes is integrated in the military structure of Central Europe. An armed conflict in this area will most probably spill over into Danish territory. NATO planning also envisages that Denmark be defended by, among others, the 6th German Armored Infantry Division stationed in Schleswig-Holstein and by German navy and air force units. Allied reinforcements are thus already and permanently present in the region in the shape of Bundeswehr units.

Denmark's own defense efforts in recent years have given Moscow both reason to rejoice and ground for concern. Over a ten-year period, real defense spending has grown only very slightly and it looks as though it might decline in the future.

NATO partners have reacted strongly and talked about "Denmarkization" as a dangerous disease in the West. NATO spokesmen must observe a delicate balance, though, in their statements. On one hand, tough reminders are made that Denmark might become "disqualified from receiving NATO reinforcements" (General Rogers). On the other hand, caution is exercised not to encourage neutralist trends in Danish public opinion by threats of non-support in wartime. A result of lax Danish defense efforts has been that German armed forces are being strengthened, since they will be called upon to shoulder a greater part of the burden in the defense of the Baltic approaches. New submarines and fast missile boats, as well as two wings of Tornado aircraft, have been added to the West German arsenal. A larger role for the German military might mean more important posts for German officers in the NATO commands of the region. Traditionally, Moscow has shown great sensitivity to such military-political developments. The attitude today remains the same, although the nervous reactions of the early 1960s are not likely to be repeated. Thus, Denmark's defense stand also has a bearing on the security of other Nordic countries.

Denmark controls the straits between the Baltic and the North Sea, and thus occupies a strategic position which has often been cited by Moscow as cause for special political prudence. The outlets from the Baltic, however, may have become less important for Moscow in recent years. The number of Soviet submarines and destroyers which would need to leave the Baltic has been gradually reduced. Most Soviet ships needed elsewhere presumably would have got out before a war started and would return for repair only in the case of a long conventional conflict. The straits can be easily and repeatedly mined from the air. Control of the outlets would require costly and difficult operations to get access not only to Denmark but also to southern Norway. Thus it has been questioned how important a choke-point the Danish straits now really are (Bjol, p. 35). Others point out the key role of the straits in the mastery of the North Sea, including control over troop and arms transports to

North Sea ports and the need for NATO forces to pass through
them in efforts to prevent Warsaw Pact forces from using the
Baltic as a transport and base area. The varying degrees of
military importance attached to the straits is due in large
measure to different estimations of the duration of the
hypothetical war. A more detailed discussion of Soviet military
positions in the Baltic is given above.

More attention has been given recently to the importance of
Danish airspace both for NATO and for the Warsaw Pact
countries. It is being argued that in order to circumvent strong
air defense systems in Central Europe, both sides might want to
send their aircraft, bombers, or cruise missiles over Danish
airspace. For NATO, Denmark has become a forward defense
area of increasing importance as the new generation of Soviet
strike aircraft acquire a much longer range. Concurrently, a
related idea gains ground in Western military discussions, namely
that seizure and exploitation of airfields in southern Norway
promise Soviet forces operational benefits of great potential
significance in a conventional war in Europe. A scenario is
painted involving a major arms thrust from the eastern Baltic
through Denmark and southern Sweden into southern Norway.
The object would be to turn these airfields into forward bases
for fighters, fighter-bombers, and bombers which would mount
strikes against air, air defense, and ground forces on the Central
front from the flank and in the rear. Access to those airfields
would also put Soviet forces in a better position to contest
control over the Norwegian and North Seas and thus to sever the
main air and sea lines of communication linking NATO's
battlefield forces with their strategic rear. Whatever credence is
being given to such speculation about Soviet military planning,
it is clear that a buildup of NATO air capacity in the region is
also taking place.

NORWAY

Norway occupies the key military-strategic position in Northern
Europe. No doubt this is the main reason for the special atten-

tion given to this country by Soviet media. Another is the abundance of natural resources found in the seabed around Norway.

Anastas Mikoyan, during a visit to Norway in the early 1960s, lamented:

> Since Arild's days, more than a thousand years ago, Norwegians and Russians have lived peacefully together up in the North. . . . Russia was the first country to recognize Norway's independence in 1905 and soon thereafter gave its guarantee of Norway's territory and integrity, a promise always scrupulously adhered to. . . . It is sad indeed that Norway joined NATO. The peaceful Norwegian people should have kept out of this aggressive body!

In recent years the tone has sharpened. "An anti-Soviet arch of crisis is being created in the North," warned *Pravda* on 19 February 1980, in reference to Norway and its policies of cooperation with NATO Allies. The list of accusations was long and detailed and had been repeated many times over, particularly since the late 1970s. The campaign intensified in 1980 when stress was placed on the dangers for other Nordic countries. Moscow argues that "Norway is gradually giving in to NATO pressure as the Americans push a new offensive strategy on their Northern flank." The public message is that while the situation in Northern Europe was stable and peaceful all through the postwar crises in East-West relations, U.S. and NATO policies in the far North now involve the whole region in international tension.

Oslo does not deny that closer links have been forged with NATO, but it claims that this is due to the buildup of Soviet strength in the area and that it represents no departure from the base and nuclear policies long pursued by Norway. It seems that in private discussions Soviet officials show a greater understanding of the Norwegian defense posture than their propaganda spokesmen.

The Strategic Picture

Increasing reliance on submarine-launched ballistic missiles (SLBMs) for strategic deterrence has transformed the North Atlantic from an area of low-level tension and militarization controlled by the West to a region of high superpower competition. The Soviet Union has concentrated some 60 percent of its SLBM forces in its Northern Fleet, based on the Kola Peninsula, the world's largest complex of naval bases. This small, ice-free area adjacent to the Soviet-Norwegian border provides the U.S.S.R. with its only naval and air bases accessible to the Atlantic. The Pacific Fleet in the Vladivostok area has in recent years been expanded so that the Northern Fleet carries less exclusive but still predominant responsibility. In the future, the Arctic Ocean will be used as an operational area for submarines. During the 1970s, the composition of the SLBM forces shifted from the medium-range SSN6 to the long-range SSN8, SSN18, and SSN20 ballistic missiles, which will permit most of the Soviet fleet to stay within range of targets in North America without leaving their home waters or the fjords and bays along the Kola Peninsula. The fleet will thus be able to avoid the dangerous passage through the well-guarded Greenland-Iceland-United Kingdom (GIUK) gap.

As the Norwegian, Greenland, and Barents Seas became patrol zones for these Soviet submarines, the Americans built up their forces to monitor them and to compete for control of these newly important strategic waters. In the relative balance of strength there, the U.S. dominates in terms of sea-based air power, with its several aircraft carriers, anti-submarine detection and warfare capacity, and the availability, at least south of the GIUK gap, of bases and facilities for aircraft and navy vessels. The Keflavik air base on Iceland dominates the whole North Atlantic area as "an unsinkable aircraft carrier." The Soviet navy so far dominates in the northern part of the Norwegian Sea and in the Barents Sea within the range of the land-based air cover that can be provided from the Kola bases. The tactical aircraft based on the Kola Peninsula have limited range, however, and will not be able to protect units of the Soviet surface fleet trying to exit the Norwegian Sea. The buildup of the Soviet navy in the 1960s and 1970s extended its control in the Norwegian Sea and raised fears in Norway and elsewhere that seaborne reinforcements from the West would be imperiled. The supersonic Backfire bomber in the Northern and the Baltic fleets was also seen as a major potential threat to the U.S. carrier forces or convoys in the Atlantic and to NATO installations in the North Atlantic area. The more recent naval buildup by the U.S., and its declared intention to conduct anti-submarine operations in the Norwegian Sea and possibly also in the Barents Sea and to keep Soviet installations on the Kola Peninsula under threat from carrier-based aircraft, created apprehensions of a direct U.S.-Soviet confrontation, of reciprocal Soviet escalation, and of the establishment of a forward Soviet *cordon sanitaire* in Norway.

Protection of the Kola complex, which in addition to the strategic submarines also houses the Northern Fleet with seventy major surface vessels, 130 attack submarines, and a host of missiles, aircraft, and radar installations, all on a fairly narrow coastal strip, requires that Norwegian territory be denied to NATO for aggressive purposes. No doubt this Soviet force is also capable of seizing and holding an appreciable territorial buffer zone to protect the base complex (John Erickson, *The Northern Theater*, p. 2). Soviet air power based on Kola has been strengthened in recent years, but the attack aircraft stationed there do not seem to be intended for short-range missions. The Soviet ground forces in that region are limited in size (30,000 to 40,000 men) and the numbers have remained fairly stable for two decades, although they have of course been given considerably better equipment.

Norway has only two peacetime garrisons in Finnmark, the Norwegian province bordering the U.S.S.R. These 1,500 men are charged mainly with border surveillance duties. An active-duty heavy brigade of 5,000 men is stationed in southern Troms, a good distance from the border. Norway can mobilize another brigade within forty-eight hours, and after full mobilization five brigades or 80,000 men are available. Added to that would come Allied reinforcements, mainly British and American Marine Corps units. There are some twenty airports in northern Norway. The most important defense installations are found in southern Troms behind the Lyngen mountains, where tough resistance can be mounted. Bowman and other Western analysts point out that a land campaign in this difficult terrain would have even greater disadvantages for the Soviets than they faced in their 1939 war with Finland, particularly because they would be limited in the number of divisions that could be spared from the Central front.

The Soviet Union's overriding interest in the Norwegian waters is generally assumed to be protection of its missile-carrying submarines and the valuable Kola base complex. This defensive task also has, of course, offensive ingredients. It is important to be able to attack Western submarines and carrier groups in the North Atlantic which threaten the Soviet SSBN "bastion." The Barents Sea off the Murmansk coast is shallow and does not offer adequate protection for large submarines. That adds to the need to have basing possibilities in the Norwegian Sea, the Greenland Sea, and part of the Arctic Ocean. Control over the Norwegian Sea and farther out to the GIUK gap is thus essential. At the very least, this large area must be denied to the enemy. Mastery of the airspace seems to be crucial to the fulfillment of these tasks.

Added to the task of protecting the Kola complex and the missile-carrying submarines is the need to protect other Soviet territory from carrier-based strikes. More aggressive goals might include penetration and destruction of the extensive American system of anti-submarine barriers in the GIUK gap to permit passage of short-range SLBMs and to cut Western sea lines of communication. Given the present capabilities on both sides and the increased Soviet emphasis on long-range SLBMs-- and presuming that the Soviets do not believe that a conflict will be a long drawn-out conventional war in which sea lines of communication would be of great interest--these latter objectives are sometimes given low priority by Western analysts (Jacobsen).

Bowman and others emphasize that even in a short conventional war "the battle of the Atlantic" would be a critical determinant in subsequent peace negotiations if it appeared that Soviet submarines and naval aircraft could close the Atlantic to the shipment of supplies and equipment from the United States to sustain NATO much beyond thirty days. Access to Norwegian airfields and possibly also to Swedish ones would be an important asset in achieving air control of the North Atlantic.

The deep-water fjords of northern Norway could provide dispersed naval basing for Soviet vessels some 1,000 nautical miles closer to the Atlantic. Soviet submarines, surface warships, and naval aircraft operating from northern Norway could greatly influence any sea battle for this region.

Estimates thus vary about the military value of Norwegian territory and bases to the Soviets. Analysts of Soviet military thinking, such as Erickson and Jacobsen, stress that the Soviet strategic imperative in northern Norway is to exclude it from active participation in hostile strategic designs. The benefits to be derived from access to northern Norway's fjords have diminished as developments in nuclear weaponry have lessened the need for additional naval bases, and the Kola Peninsula has proved to satisfy added requirements. Provided that Norwegian territory remained "neutral," the Soviets would gain little defensively by moving their bases westward against tough Norwegian resistance, according to these observers. Dissenting views are expressed by, for example, the U.S. secretary of the navy, who claims that "the Soviets' current strategy is to take Norway very early and operate their submarines out of the Norwegian fjords" (Bjol, p. 21). Other Western analysts (MccGwire) state that control of the Norwegian Sea is a high priority for defense of the SSBN bastions, which would be greatly facilitated by control of the adjoining Norwegian coast and its air bases and ports.

The repeated submarine intrusions into Norwegian waters are often cited as added proof of Soviet preparations for such operations. Soviet naval exercises in the northeast Atlantic and the Norwegian Sea have also demonstrated massive capabilities and evoked concern among Western observers. In July 1985, large units from the Soviet Northern, Baltic, and Black Sea navies simulated naval and air battles with "Western" forces off the coast of mid-Norway in the region between Iceland and Ireland.

Concurrently, Soviet submarines appeared to form four barriers, one between North Cape and Spitzbergen, the second from the coastal island of Lofoten in northern Norway to Jan Mayen, the third from Scotland to the southern coast of Norway, and the fourth between Scotland and Iceland. Western military observers assumed that the aim of the exercise was to show how American battle groups could be defeated south of the GIUK gap and how Soviet supremacy could be established in the Norwegian Sea. Amphibious exercises were also conducted, stimulating concern over possible plans for attacks on Norway. NATO's response came a few months later with a major exercise, Ocean Safari '85, involving almost 160 naval units from eight NATO countries, principally the U.S., showing a firm ambition to project large naval and air power in these waters close to the Kola base area.

Another aspect of particular interest to Sweden is the general Western belief that it would be in Soviet interests to make quick air strikes on Norwegian air bases and ports very early in a conflict to prevent the arrival of Allied reinforcements. The shortest route for such attacks would be over Swedish territory. Soviet naval aircraft would also gain by overflying Swedish airspace to attack NATO forces in the Atlantic. Thus, Swedish air defense capabilities are important to the Western Allies as a shield for Norway and the Atlantic, and to the U.S.S.R. as protection against cruise missiles from the North Atlantic.

There are a number of Western studies and reports outlining the Soviet interest in controlling parts of both Sweden and Norway in conjunction with a battle in the North Atlantic. The gains are fairly clearly defined, although opinions differ on how important they might be in various scenarios, but the costs of such operations are discussed less often. Nuclear deterrence might not be effective when there is equivalency in nuclear strategic capability, and indeed Soviet military doctrine assumes that a major war in Europe can be kept conventional. However, the deployment of conventional forces in the North and the geographical factors render a conventional attack on Sweden and Norway fairly unattractive.

An informed Western observer, after a careful review of Soviet conventional options in the North, concluded in an optimistic vein:

> The pattern of Soviet options and geomilitary constraints on the northern flank does not offer any real opportunities for Soviet success. Harassment is counterproductive; local attack on northern Norway would be defeated with heavy military and political losses for the Soviets; an attack on the northern flank as part of a general attack on NATO could be turned back with minimum levels of reinforcement; an attack through Sweden would produce a relatively stronger force balance in favor of the Alliance; and a direct attack on southern Norway would be impractical as long as Alliance defenses succeeded in the central region.
>
> The enduring Alliance problem for the future is to maintain this favorable system of constraints on Soviet options, in spite of the steady improvements in Soviet forces. Effective coordination of Alliance defense efforts, together with effective use of new technology for improving our ability to detect and destroy intruding enemy forces, should ensure continued successful deterrence on the northern flank. (Bowman, *Armed Forces Journal International*, vol. 121, no. 9 (April 1984).)

It can also be argued that it would be important for the Russians to keep the Kola bases out of a conflict for as long as possible. A Soviet attack on northern Norway could very well trigger a massive counterattack directed against this strategic region.

Norwegian Restraints

Norwegians (and Danes) have long observed certain restraints in their military posture to cater to the security interests of the U.S.S.R. Sometimes these policies were adopted because Soviet protests or pressures brought about a better understanding of these security interests; sometimes, the policies simply resulted from considerations of what would best serve peace and stability in the Nordic region. Positions on foreign bases or nuclear weapons have been defined after considerable domestic political debate in which the parties to the left, particularly, have argued prudence and restraint.

In 1951, Soviet protests provoked the Oslo government to specify its base policy. It was then made clear that the base policy would not prevent Norway from

- putting its bases at the disposal of Allied troops in case of an attack on the North Atlantic region or at any time that Norwegian authorities considered Norway to be threatened;

- preparing for such situations by entering into conditional agreements with the Allies;

- building military installations so that they would be suitable for receiving and supporting Allied troops sent to aid in the defense of Norway; and

- participating in Allied maneuvers or exercises or receiving Allied air or naval forces on short visits.

In 1977-78, the Norwegian government made some additional rulings on the application of its base policy in the light of experience during these years. It was then decided that the base policy would allow Allied troops to go to Norway for short exercises or in connection with Allied maneuvers in preparation for activity in Norway; permit guidance, surveillance, warning, or similar installations to be set up in Norway to serve Allied needs; and allow depots to be constructed for the stockpiling of ammunition and other equipment for Allied troops. In addition, it was determined that

Norway's base policy would not prevent Norway from participating fully in integrated NATO military operations, including subordinating Norwegian troops to Allied command, allowing the Allies to set up staff commands in Norway, and allowing Norwegians to participate in these commands.

Within this formal framework, a pattern of military restraints has developed over the years which has not been officially defined in all its details. These "confidence-building measures" are confidential and can therefore be changed more easily according to need or as a means of retaliation or pressure. The underlying principle is that Norway decides on its own what restraints it will apply to its military policy and does not bind itself with international or formal arrangements.

Norway does not allow Allied land-force exercises in the northeastern province of Finnmark, which keeps Allied forces at a distance of some 800 kilometers by road from the Soviet border. Allied military aircraft are not permitted in Norwegian airspace beyond the 24th east meridian, and normally the same meridian is the limit for Allied naval vessels. Partly as a confidence-building measure, partly for purely military reasons, Norway maintains only a small force in the border region of Finnmark and has concentrated its defense of the north farther away in the province of Troms. For similar reasons, it decided in 1981 to stockpile equipment for a U.S. Marine amphibious brigade (MAB) in central Norway instead of in the north as planned.

Norway's policy on nuclear weapons was most succinctly presented in 1981 by the Labor party defense minister:

> Norwegian nuclear policy implies that nuclear weapons will not be stockpiled or stationed in Norway. In contrast to what is the case with the base policy, no statement has been made that the policy is only valid as long as Norway is not under attack or threat of an attack. The policy is defined by the practice followed since the parliamentary decision in 1961. Thus . . . there have been no preparations to receive or use nuclear weapons in crises or war. . . .

> Norwegian forces are not trained to use nuclear
> weapons. There are no special installations to
> receive nuclear weapons in wartime. We have not
> made preparations for the special communication
> network necessary for the use of nuclear
> weapons. Norway has not concluded any
> agreement with the United States regarding
> nuclear weapons. Defense plans for our country
> foresee a conventional defense.

In 1978 the Defense Commission of the Norwegian Parliament made some other clarifications of this policy, which were slightly different in tone. The commission stated that in times of war Norwegian troops could be supported by Allied forces equipped with nuclear weapons; that Norwegian forces could use nuclear weapons in defense of their country; that Norwegian forces could be equipped to protect themselves against nuclear weapons and could participate in exercises for the purpose of such protection; that foreign warships visiting Norwegian ports could carry nuclear weapons, even if previous Norwegian governmental policy was that they should not; and that certain Norwegian installations could be set up to receive aircraft and ships equipped with nuclear weapons, provided that this did not imply the stationing of foreign forces or nuclear weapons on Norwegian territory in peacetime.

Soviet Complaints

The Soviets have over the years shown their very active interest in expanding Norwegian commitments to restraint, and they have also tried to establish some kind of bilateral consultation procedure on these problems as well as on other Northern issues.

Special attention has been given to Svalbard. The Soviets have made numerous proposals--all of which have been rejected--regarding Svalbard, including that Norway and the U.S.S.R. jointly build an airport on the island, that declarations be signed on the unique role of the U.S.S.R. and Norway in this area, and that the two countries formally agree to consult regularly on this question, thus precluding any unilateral Norwegian administrative decision concerning Svalbard. Moscow has stressed the "demilitarized status" granted to Svalbard by the 1920 treaty and has objected to Norwegian activities on the island which Moscow deemed to be of a paramilitary nature. A series of skirmishes between Oslo and Moscow took place in the 1970s over the Svalbard issue. One long-time Norwegian foreign minister concluded:

> These episodes were not the result of Soviet expansion that Norway had to suffer. If anything the contrary was true. After a long period of passivity on the part of various Norwegian governments, the authorities finally started to exercise full control over Svalbard. Soviet policy was aimed at maintaining the earlier situation. (K. Frydenlund, *Lilleland: hva na?*, Oslo, 1982.)

Soviet complaints about Norway's defense policy centered on military installations, nuclear weapons, and missiles, but in more recent times they have also included and emphasized Norwegian "services" to the United States, such as electronic surveillance, intelligence, and the joint exercises and maneuvers in northern Norway. The borderline between bona fide declarations of concern and tactical statements made to pressure and obtain extra advantages is difficult to establish.

Recent Soviet accusations stress the general theme that "Washington is obsessed with plans for the so-called strengthening of NATO's Northern flank" and that therefore Norway is being pressured into schemes that entail danger for Sweden and Finland. In contrast, "the U.S.S.R. has not taken and is not taking any actions aimed at complicating the situation in this part of Europe. In recent years, the Soviet Union has refrained from holding any large-scale maneuvers in immediate proximity to the borders of the North European states" (*Izvestija*, 24 January 1981)--an excessively modest appraisal of Soviet naval activities in the North. Specifically, the following themes have been put forth by the Soviets.

The first theme concerns the "prepositioning agreement," that is, the Norwegian-American agreement on stockpiling arms and equipment "to arm a U.S. brigade of 10,000 men to be dispatched if Washington deems that a crisis situation has heightened tension in the Nordic area," as the Russians put it. Numerous articles describe this agreement as the equivalent of base facilities (*Pravda*, 19 February 1980: "every foreign military strongpoint is in effect a base"). Some articles also claim that the U.S. Marines will prepare airfields for use by F-111 bombers armed with nuclear weapons, supplementing the INF deployed in Central Europe; others maintain that the pre-stocked equipment will include "artillery systems that have been adapted to use nuclear ammunition" (*Izvestija*, 24 January 1981). The general argument goes that the original Norwegian base policy is being continually and incrementally eroded by such measures, and that the bases are actually intended for foreign NATO troops and are manned only temporarily by Norwegians. For long parts of the year, these bases are used for large exercises by foreign troops. Soviet criticism is particularly directed against the large air capacity foreseen in the prepositioning agreement.

The Norwegians, who have conducted bilateral consultations with Moscow on this subject, claim that increased Soviet capacity to interdict seaborne transportation across the Atlantic has required reinforcement measures, more regular exercises of Allied troops in Norway, and pre-stocking of heavy equipment and ammunition. In fact, these measures also reduce the pressure on Norway to permit the permanent stationing of foreign forces and, more importantly, reduce the need to call for reinforcements in the early stage of a crisis. (A few days will be sufficient to fly in the U.S. Marine Corps brigade when arrangements are ready in the late 1980s.) As to nuclear weapons carriers, practically all modern aircraft and the large artillery systems in question are equipped for dual use. The Russians have declared themselves totally unconvinced by these arguments.

The fundamental issue in wartime is air superiority in Norwegian airspace and the ability to operate aircraft from Norwegian bases to protect transatlantic sea lines of communication. Agreements have been in existence since the 1950s on the storage of spare parts and ammunition for Allied aircraft. These agreements have been extended to cover the emergency evacuation of U.S. carrier-based aircraft and the possible transfer of Allied fighter squadrons, mainly F-16s, to eight designated airfields in Norway in times of crisis or war (the COB program). The Soviet charge that these arrangements imply preparation for the use of Norway as a staging point for nuclear-equipped aircraft is clearly at variance with the stated purpose.

The U.S.-Norwegian agreement regarding pre-stocking for a marine amphibious brigade with a large aviation element includes 155 millimeter howitzers which are designed for dual use. No warheads or equipment for nuclear use are stockpiled in Norway. The clear purpose of the arrangement was to enhance the capacity for the conventional defense of Norway, and the storage site was changed from the north to central Norway partly in deference to Soviet sensitivities. Oslo, of course, claims that the call for reinforcements would be made by Norway, and not, as Moscow says, by the United States.

The Soviets may have noted this relative restraint, but they show no signs in their media of having done so. The overall analysis seems to remain that Norway has been further integrated into a NATO structure which is acquiring a more aggressive posture. On the other hand, the arrangements for the next decade are now fairly well established. Soviet criticism of similar events in the past has subsided; perhaps this matter will also come to rest.

NATO planners might be tempted to install conventional weapons of high accuracy in Norway to be aimed at targets on the Kola Peninsula. The Norwegians, however, are likely to consider carefully any potentially destabilizing move which would not be warranted by their defense interests.

The second Soviet theme is that Norway's nuclear policy is being circumvented in practice. The Russians argue that Norway's nuclear delivery systems (F-104 and Starfighter attack planes, anti-aircraft guided missile systems, dual-use howitzers, etc.) compromise that policy. Allied warships and aircraft armed with nuclear weapons make stops in Norway as part of exercises on patrol. The U.S. policy of neither denying nor confirming the presence of nuclear weapons on their ships or planes is referred to as proof that the Norwegian government does not necessarily know what is going on. Unilateral proclamations thus have little value. A non-nuclear status must be backed by NATO commitments to respect that non-nuclear status. The Russians stress that while Norway or Denmark might not feel the need for any nuclear defense capability of their own, the Americans regard their territory as a suitable strong-point in the U.S. nuclear strategy. To these arguments the Norwegians reply that while they do indeed possess dual-use weapons, these weapons are not equipped nor will they be used with nuclear munitions until after a Norwegian decision to go nuclear. Because of the solidarity within the Alliance, Oslo has no reason to believe that it is being fooled by its American ally or that its territory is being unduly exploited.

The Russians retort that in crises and war military decisions will be made by NATO's Northern Command according to defense plans worked out beforehand. Those plans have been approved by the Norwegian authorities and surely contain the option of nuclear use. Whatever decision-making process is foreseen, the Russians are apt to suspect or even to assume that the NATO Command will use nuclear weapons if it finds that there are sufficient military and political reasons to do so. No doubt Moscow plans for the worst-case scenarios.

The third Soviet theme consists of accusations that NATO intelligence activities in northern Norway linked to U.S. strategic forces are being stepped up. According to *Pravda* (22 November 1980), that area is "the focal point for electronic espionage against the U.S.S.R.," containing eleven stations that survey Soviet aircraft, ships, and radio communications. "Two

Loran-S and Omega radio navigation stations (and eight more planned) operate in Norway serving American submarines in the northern Atlantic carrying nuclear weapons" (*Tass*, 6 January 1982, and *Izvestija*, 24 January 1981). These submarines call at Norwegian ports. AWACS aircraft are serviced at Evenes Air Base with no Norwegian control over the data collected, and these intelligence aircraft will in the future depart from Norway's Oerland airstation.

The Norwegian version is different. In 1977, the Norwegian government made an official interpretation of its base policy in which it stated, among other things, that this policy "does not prevent the establishment on Norwegian territory of installations for command, control, communications, navigation, warning, etc., for Allied forces." This broad mandate still seemed to carry restrictions, for instance that Norway would not permit the peacetime integration of Norwegian radar facilities into U.S. strategic submarine targeting designs. The Loran and Omega stations which were set up in the 1950s and 1960s are said to be serving merely as a general navigational aid. Norwegian critics, on the other hand, have maintained that U.S. nuclear submarines do need to use these installations. In any case, whatever importance they might now have will be lost when NAVSTAR, the new satellite navigation system, becomes operational. E-3A planes, whose range includes the Murmansk area, do indeed take off and land from the Oerland airfield, which was designated as a forward operating base for the NATO Airborne Early Warning Force, but Norway controls its plan of operations, limits flight routes, etc. The Norwegians do not deny that they conduct considerable tactical electronic and other surveillance of Soviet military developments in border areas, including checking the movements of Soviet submarines via a SOSUS line between Bear Island and Finnmark. Indeed, they stress that precisely in order to reduce the danger of direct great-power confrontation in the airspace close to Soviet bases, Norwegian maritime patrol aircraft have assumed primary responsibility for surveillance of the Barents Sea.

Presumably a distinction can be made between general intelligence, which improves warning times, on one hand, and, on the other hand, surveillance that is directly integrated into hostile strategic systems, such as nuclear-armed submarines. One authority on the subject, John Erickson, emphasizes that "Moscow cannot accept that contiguous Norwegian territory is used in a manner inimical to Soviet security interests-- particularly radar or other surveillance systems as well as missile or anti-missile capabilities." In another American study, an analysis is made which shows some understanding for the Soviet case (B. Posen, *International Security*, vol. 7, no. 2). Referring to U.S. Navy and administration arguments in favor of forward anti-submarine warfare operations and attacks with conventionally armed, carrier-based aircraft against naval bases and forces in the Kola area, Posen paints an ominous picture of the possible consequences of Norwegian policy. Norwegian air bases are well situated for conducting air strikes against Kola. Intelligence-gathering facilities located in northern Norway allow NATO to plot the movements of Soviet aircraft, surface vessels, and submarines. The sonar array in the Bear Island gap allows the Norwegians to monitor the movements of Soviet submarines in the Barents Sea region. Land-based radar tracks the Northern Fleet's air arm, forcing it to fly evasive flight patterns. Communications of Northern Fleet headquarters are monitored by facilities near the border. All this provides the West with substantial early warning of Soviet military preparations. In case of war, this information will be provided to NATO naval forces. Thus, the air base structure and intelligence-gathering facilities in northern Norway could be construed by the Soviets to be (and could well be) an offensive threat to Soviet control of the Barents Sea. These facilities would aid any NATO air, surface, subsurface, or combined offensive against the Northern Fleet and its bases. Consequently, says Posen, elimination of NATO capabilities would appear attractive to the Soviets.

Norwegian officials reject the implied criticism in the above analysis. They argue that reciprocal restraint is necessary and that in this respect the U.S.S.R. is found lacking, among other things by its buildup in the Kola area. Early warning is essential for Norway's own defense preparations. Talk about an American offensive capacity in the Norwegian Sea is exaggerated given the limited resources available and the divided opinions about the use of carriers in this area. Norway is in any case part of the Atlantic Alliance and the Russians cannot dictate the framework of its membership.

The three areas under Soviet scrutiny--preparations for Allied reinforcements and the base policy, the nuclear policy, and the installations in northern Norway for intelligence and reconnaissance--are crucial for Norwegian security and for Norway's membership in the Atlantic Alliance. Technical developments and the Soviet buildup have obliged the Norwegians to make some moves toward further integration into NATO. In the nuclear field, however, the evolution of public opinion and of Labor party policies goes in the other direction.

The assistance that Norway can give to the Allies in the field of intelligence is reciprocated by the promise of aid that it receives. Norway is dependent on NATO for its defense, but it is of interest to the Alliance in large part because of the strategic services it can render. The Soviet concern stems precisely from this situation. The Norwegians have experience in muddling through. The increased attention given to their area will make even more necessary a balanced and prudent policy in the future.

Oil, Gas, and Security

The strategic situation in the North and Soviet policies in the region are obviously affected by the existence of large gas and oil resources off both southern and northern Norway and within the area covered by the Svalbard Treaty. The Troll field off southern Norway is now regarded as one of the world's largest off-shore gas fields. It could satisfy Western Europe's entire demand for natural gas for a decade if--and it is a big if--the costs of exploiting these fields, which are situated in very deep waters, could be met. Because gas from this area will be more expensive than, for example, Soviet gas, consumers will probably have to pay a "political security premium."

Off northern Norway toward Bear Island and into the Svalbard area, there are fields of petroleum which so far, because of the hostile environment and the great depths, have not proven commercially interesting. Exploration is underway, however, and it is possible that fixed installations might be set up in great numbers in this strategic region. Moscow's concern is understandable, both for strategic and for economic reasons.

Not surprisingly, there is a legal dispute between Norway and the U.S.S.R. regarding this important and sensitive region. Norway argues that the Svalbard Treaty applies only to the land area of the islands and the territorial waters immediately surrounding them. Norway refers to the 1958 Geneva Treaty and argues that Svalbard does not have its own continental shelf and that Norway's shelf stretches from the Finnmark coastline up to north of Svalbard. The Soviet Union has explicitly rejected the Norwegian interpretaion, and Norway's allies, the United States and the United Kingdom, have reserved their positions as to Oslo's reading of the treaty.

The Barents Sea

The conflict between Norway and the Soviet Union over the partition line in the Barents Sea complicates the situation in the North. Negotiations have been conducted since 1970 without results. Oslo maintains that the median line between the two shores should divide the territories. Moscow argues for the sector principle, saying that a line should be drawn from the point on the shore where the land borders of the two countries meet toward the North Pole. The difference between the two is 155,000 square kilometers of sea territory, as large as Norway's share of the North Sea continental shelf. Moscow's case rests not only on its interpretation of international law, but also on a number of "special considerations," such as the long Soviet coastline, the large population of the Kola Peninsula, the strategic importance of the area, and so on. Its traditional position is also that all land territory and islands between the Soviet coastline and the North Pole belong to the Soviet Union.

Although negotiations so far have failed, the situation has been calm and free from tension. Both parties, however, take measures to symbolize their presence and claims. The Soviet Union conducted missile tests in international waters in the Barents Sea with target areas within the western part of the disputed region. Concurrently, Norway conducted seismic tests in the vicinity. In 1978, the two countries concluded an agreement on a so-called grey area to be placed under a form of joint jurisdiction to protect fish resources in the Barents Sea. The agreement was strongly criticized in Norway as being too favorable to the Soviets, particularly as it might prejudice any later territorial demarcation. The dispute concerns the rich fish resources and likely oil and gas deposits that can be found in the Barents Sea, but both parties have refrained from any large-scale explorations in the contested area. Norway does not have any plans in the foreseeable future to start exploitation. Soviet test-drilling has been undertaken but so far it has been confined mainly to the ice-free region north of the Murmansk coast, although there are some indications that Soviet exploitation might move westward. In the absence of agreed boundaries, disputes of some magnitude can thus arise in the future.

CONCLUSION

"We are not responsible for geography." Thus said Stalin to the Finns in 1939 when he demanded that the small neighbor cede territory in order to guarantee Soviet security. The Nordic states cannot escape the fact that they are situated next to a superpower and they must seek ways and means to live together with it.

In crises and in war, the essence of a nation's policy is put to the test. In World War II, Finland had to make a fateful choice. While the immediate issue at hand, a slice of territory, was not of major importance, the Finns defended the principle not to give up any national territory or to give in to big-power pressure, particularly since demands might thereafter grow even bigger. It is impossible to say whether any other decision would have served Finland better.

The leaders in Moscow might originally have aimed for only limited gains. Faced with opposition from this small neighboring country, however, they went for the whole lot, no doubt intending to subjugate Finland, an operation that seemed to entail few risks and low costs. They miscalculated, suffering great losses, losing prestige, and giving the real enemy a revanchist ally.

The Finns later showed that by unity, fighting spirit, luck, and international prestige, a small country can manage to save its existence against all odds. After the war, a policy of accommodation mixed with stubborn but prudent determination to safeguard its national independence has created a modus vivendi with the neighboring superpower.

Today, the situation in Europe is entirely different from the time preceding the Second World War. Nuclear weapons make the borderline between East and West so dangerously sensitive that efforts to change it by armed force would only be undertaken by reckless gamblers. The zones outside the power blocs are likewise protected by the excessive risks an attack would entail and by the apparent interest on both sides to maintain the status quo.

In Northern Europe there is only one region, northern Norway, which has a strategic value for the Soviet Union comparable to or greater than that which provoked the Soviet attack on Finland in 1939. The whole region, including the Soviet part, forms the military-strategic nerve center of Northern Europe and carries all the risks associated with that position. It is here that policies now require this careful balance between steadfastness and prudence, deterrence and reassurance.

Prospects for Nordic security have improved, President Kekkonen said in 1965, referring to new dimensions of international politics and military strategy. The Nordic region did not figure in any international conflict. The risk of escalation to a cataclysm prevented wars in Europe. Several new factors contributed to make Northern Europe less militarily important than before. Wars would be started and conducted by missiles fired far away from their targets. Observation satellites took care of reconnaissance. Wars were no longer conducted by moving troops, aircraft, or ships within a given geographical region. Thus, neighboring regions were not necessary for defensive or offensive purposes. Bases and territory in general had lost in importance.

In part, Kekkonen's positive appraisal of Nordic security prospects still appears to be justified. Wars in Europe seem even more unlikely than they did twenty years ago. What is more uncertain is the validity of his appraisal of Northern Europe's military importance in the unlikely event of such an armed conflict. Geography might not be so important as it was in World War II, but a buffer zone or a forward terrain is still useful. Flexible response means planning for a drawn-out conventional war. Cruise missiles and more sophisticated aircraft increase the need for advanced quick alert and air defense systems. In addition, there is the increased strategic significance of the North Atlantic and the value of Swedish and Norwegian territory in controlling this region.

Strategic developments also create trouble in peacetime. Nordic security might be endangered by the increased threat to vital installations in the northwestern U.S.S.R. posed by cruise missiles fired from aircraft, surface ships, and submarines over the Nordic region. This could increase the Soviet military's desire to plan for an extension of their air defense zone in Northern Europe. Improvement in aircraft capacity is likewise a problem. Strikes against enemy naval forces in the Atlantic can now be undertaken by Soviet tactical aircraft, whose capability would be greatly improved by flying over Nordic airspace. NATO might likewise want to attack targets in the northwestern U.S.S.R. via Swedish airspace. It can be argued, though, that these new military factors are simply successors to old problems which were equally disturbing for Nordic security.

The balance of power in the air and on the sea has shifted, possibly increasing the risks for neutral Sweden. The Swedish air force has declined in numbers while Soviet aircraft have increased in range, and contingency plans have been made for the rapid transfer of large American air force units to Denmark and Norway. While Sweden earlier was able to defend its own airspace against any intruder, this might not be the case in the future. Likewise, in the Baltic Sweden's "buffer defense" capacity has declined relative to Warsaw Pact and NATO forces. While this does not, per se, increase the risks of war, violations of Swedish territory in an armed conflict will cost an aggressor less.

The national defense efforts of the Nordic countries and their reliance on military help from others will play an important role in the stability of the region. Norway and Denmark are increasing their integration into NATO and take measures to facilitate speedy Allied reinforcements in a crisis. Norwegian defense expenditures will rise by 3.5 percent in real terms each year for the next five years. On the other hand, Denmark's real defense spending may decline in the next few years. Finland has substantially increased its armed forces during recent years within the restrictions imposed by a defense budget of only 1.6 percent of GNP.

Sweden has spent very considerable resources on national defense during the entire postwar period and has produced highly sophisticated arms and equipment. For ten years, however, spending has stagnated at a lower level necessitating cut-backs in the services. In the future, submarine incursions and a chillier international climate might combine to effect an increase in spending, at least in those parts of the defense forces that should handle incursions and other violations of Swedish territory in peacetime as well as in war.

Those and other military developments are clearly important when discussing the conflict potential in the North, but they do not in themselves initiate wars. Political factors are instrumental. The relationship between the superpowers, the evolution of Soviet and East European internal situations, escalation of strategic Third World conflicts, etc., are the crucial variables for Nordic security.

A mixture of competition and cooperation, suspicion and a modicum of trust, aggressiveness and prudence will probably, as before, characterize the relationship between the superpowers, which is bound to remain tense after a decade of almost constant disputes following a short-lived detente. As of now, both parties seem determined to maintain a prudent posture in crises so as to avoid direct confrontations. Whatever has preserved peace during the last decades--deterrence, parity, support for the status quo, or the absence of demands for dramatic change--might very well continue to work for the foreseeable future. No great shifts in the power relationship can be seen on the horizon. There is no evidence that the U.S.S.R. has embarked upon any new policy, either offensively or defensively. Thus, in this regard the Nordic area might be able to maintain its relative stability.

Transatlantic relations are the subject of continuous debate in the West, and they fluctuate. Under Reagan, Washington has tried to reassert U.S. leadership over the Western Alliance, which has been contested but also accepted by Europeans, who have other economic and political interests but who are also vitally interested in maintaining the American presence and protection. Many observers foresee a gradual American military withdrawal from Europe for reasons having to do with economics, a shift of American interests to the Pacific, a belief on both sides of the Atlantic in the capacity of Europeans to defend themselves, and so on. The Scandinavian NATO members might then come to rely more on Western European rather than American support. Sweden has a vital interest in a continued balance of strength between East and West and in maintaining a situation in Europe which does not encourage aggression.

Closer Western European military cooperation has been talked about for some time, but acted upon only on a modest scale. In the absence of radical change in transatlantic relations or of an East-West crisis, development in this regard will probably be slow. It is hard to see that this would have any substantial influence on the Nordic countries' security situation.

Soviet behavior in Northern Europe, of course, has parallels elsewhere in areas of interest to the U.S.S.R. In its own sphere, harsh control is the rule. In other regions, an opportunistic policy consisting of probings and efforts to expand power positions combined with tactical retreats, all within a low-risk and low-cost framework, is the characteristic pattern. Errors of judgment and analysis are necessarily frequent. In these respects, Soviet behavior is not that different from what the policies of other great powers have been.

In Northern Europe, the situation is more stable than in any other area close to the Soviet Union. Soviet policies here are anchored in a tradition of considerable restraint. When sharp conflicts have arisen over the cooperation of the Scandinavian NATO members with Western powers, they have so far been handled with a certain mutual consideration of legitimate interests. There are no new factors in the North which radically change the conditions under which traditional Soviet policy has operated. This seems to be true as far as Western capabilities and intentions are concerned. The buildup of Soviet forces in the far North and the increasing importance of those forces within the overall context of Soviet strategic requirements might have gradually changed the military environment in this region. This does not mean however that the basic configuration of the Nordic countries' foreign and defense policies has become invalid or that Moscow thinks so. Soviet leaders would certainly prefer that the Nordic countries adopt policies more in line with Soviet interests, by, for example, creating a loose grouping of neutral states amical to the U.S.S.R., but it is aware of the formidable obstacles to change. The mixture of armed neutrality and Alliance links--deterrence and reassurance combined--is solidly anchored in the North and has stood the test of time.

SELECTED BIBLIOGRAPHY

As the title of this section indicates, this bibliography does not intend to be exhaustive or to cover all the material that has been used in the preparation of this book. Thus, for example, with one or two exceptions, I have not listed articles but have cited only books, although many articles containing valuable information and insights have been useful. Certain periodicals, in which the most important Nordic contributions on this subject are made, have been noted and the most prominent authors named within brackets. *Pravda, Izvestija, International Affairs*, and other Soviet newspapers and periodicals in the original or as translated by the Foreign Broadcast Information Service (FBIS) or *Current Report on the Soviet Union* are indeed main reference sources. General handbooks are not listed, nor have I found it necessary to refer to the general Western literature that deals with Soviet foreign policy in various respects and from different perspectives, except insofar as it pertains directly to Nordic problems. Only the most important official Nordic documents are listed.

Amstrup, N., and I. Faurby (eds.), *Studier i dansk udenrigspolitik*, Arhus, 1978.

Andren, N. (ed.), *Sakerhetspolitik i Norden*, Stockholm, 1984.

Assarsson, V., *I skuggan av Stalin*, Stockholm, 1962.

Bialer, Seweryn (ed.), *Stalin and His Generals: Soviet Military Memoirs of World War II*, New York, 1969.

Bjol, E., *Nordic Security*, Adelphi Papers 181, London, 1983.

Blechman, B., et al., *Force Without War: U.S. Armed Forces as a Political Instrument*, Washington, 1978.

Boheman, E., *Pa Vakt*, Stockholm, 1964.

Brezhnev, L., *On the Policy of the Soviet Union and the International Situation*, New York, 1983.

Biography written for Simon & Schuster under the supervision of the Soviet Academy of Science, 1978.

Brodin, K., *Finlands Utrikes-Politiska Doktrin*, Stockholm, 1971.

Carlgren, W., *Svensk Utrikespolitik 1939-45*, Stockholm, 1973.

Churchill, W., *The Second World War*, London (12 vols.).

Cooperation and Conflict (Nordic Studies in International
      Politics): Numerous articles by Brundtland, Bjol,
      Brodin, Dorfer, Holst, Sjaastad, Korhonen, Pajunen,
      Wahlback, and others.

Dallin, D., *Soviet Russia's Foreign Policy 1939-42*, New Haven,
      1942.

Dau, M., *Danmark og Sovjetunionen 1944-49*, Copenhagen,
      1969.

Davies, J., *Mission to Moscow*, London, 1945.

*Dansk sakerhetspolitik och forslagen om en nordisk karnvapenfri
      zon*, S.N.U., Copenhagen, 1982.

*Dansk Udenrigspolitisk Arbog [Yearbook of Danish Foreign
      Policy]*, Copenhagen, various years.

Degras, J., (ed.), *Soviet Documents on Foreign Policy 1933-41*,
      London, 1953.

Dedijer, Vladimir, *The Battle Stalin Lost--Memories of
      Yugoslavia 1948-53*, New York, 1976.

Djilas, M., *Conversations with Stalin*, New York, 1962.

Eden, A., *The Eden Memoirs*, London, 1965.

Erickson, J., "The Northern Theatre--Soviet Capabilities and
      Concepts," *Strategic Review*, 1976:2.

Erlander, T., *Memoirs* in four volumes.

Espersen, M., *The Baltic: Balance and Security*, Copenhagen,
      1982.

Feis, H., *Churchill, Roosevelt and Stalin: The War They Waged
      and the Peace They Sought*, Princeton, 1967.

Fiedler, H., *Der Sowjetische Neutralitats Begriff*, Cologne, 1959.

Folk och Forsvar (publ.), *Tio debattinlagg om svensk
      sakerhetspolitik*, Stockholm, 1984.

Frydenlund, K., *Lilleland: hva na?*, Oslo, 1982.

Gerhardsen, E., *Felleskap i krig og fred: Erindringer 1940-45*,
      Oslo, 1970.

      Samarbeid og strid: Erindringer 1945-55, Oslo, 1971.

Gorshkov, S., *Sea Power and the State*, New York, 1979.

Grechko, A. A., *Selected Soviet Military Writings 1970-75*, Washington, 1977.

Gromyko, A. A., and B. N. Ponomarev, *Istoria Vneshney Politiki SSSR 1945-80*, Moscow, 1980.

Grondal, B., *Iceland from Neutrality to NATO Membership*, Oslo, 1971.

Hagglof, G., *Det Kringranda Sverige*, Stockholm, 1983.

Hagglof, I., *Jag berattar for Joen--Mina ar med ryssarna*, Stockholm, 1984.

Hakalehto, I. (ed.), *Finlands utrikespolitik 1809-1966*, Stockholm, 1968.

Harpe, W., *Die Sowjetunion, Finnland und Skandinavien 1945-55*, Tuebingen, 1956.

Heurlin, B. (ed.), *Kernevapenpolitik i Norden*, Copenhagen, 1983.

Hodgson, J., *Communism in Finland: A History and Interpretation*, Princeton, 1967.

Holst, J. J., *Norsk sikkerhetspolitik i strategisk perspektiv*, I and II, Oslo, 1967.

Five Roads to Nordic Security, Oslo, 1973.

Numerous articles and studies on Norwegian and Nordic security problems in, for example, *Cooperation and Conflict*, *Internasjonal Politik*, and *NUPI Rapport*.

Internasjonal Politik (Norwegian journal of international affairs), numerous articles. See *Cooperation and Conflict*.

Internationella Studier, periodical published by the Swedish Foreign Policy Institute, Stockholm.

Jacobsen, C. G., *Soviet Strategic Initiatives*, New York, 1979.

Jagerskiold, S., biography of C. G. Mannerheim (7 vols.).

Jakobson, M., *Finnish Neutrality: A Study of Finnish Foreign Policy Since the Second World War*, New York, 1968.

The Diplomacy of the Winter War, Cambridge, Mass., 1961.

Den finlandska paradoxen, Helsinki, 1982.

Trettioattonde vaningen, Helsinki, 1983.

Kan, A. S., *Noveyshaya istoria Shvetsii*, Moscow, 1964.

Vneshnaya politika skandinaviskikh stran v gody vtoroi mirovoi voiny, Moscow, 1967.

Karvonen, *Sovetskij Soyouz i Finlandia*, with preface by Kommissarov, Moscow, 1977.

Kekkonen, U., *Brobygge Tal 1943-68*, Tammersors, 1969.

Killander, Lars, *Avskrekking og beroligelse--norsk forsvarspolitik under 80-talet*, Stockholm, 1984.

Koivisto, M., *Ramarken*, Helsinki, 1983.

Kommissarov, Y., Preface to Karvonen, *op. cit.*

Kommissarov, Y., and T. Bartenyev, *Tridtsat let Dobrososedstva*, Moscow, 1976.

Korhonen, K. (ed.), *Urho Kekkonen--A Statesman for Peace*, London, 1975.

Kuznetsov, Y., *Bezopasnost na severe Europy*, Moscow, 1967.

Lange, H., *Norsk udenrigspolitik siden 1945*, Oslo, 1952.

Norges vei til NATO, Oslo, 1966.

Lie, T., *Syv ar for Freden*, Oslo, 1954.

Loftson, E., *Island og NATO*, Copenhagen, 1981.

Lonnroth, E., *Den svenska utrikespolitikens historia 1919-1939*, Stockholm, 1959.

Lundestad, G., *America, Scandinavia and the Cold War 1945-49*, Oslo, 1980.

The American Non-Policy Toward East Europe 1943-47, Tromso, 1978.

Lundin, L., *Finland och andra varldskriget*, Ekenas, 1958.

Maisky, J., *Memoirs of a Soviet Ambassador: The War 1939-43*, London, 1967.

Mannerheim, C. G., *Minnen, I-II*, Helsinki, 1951-52.

Maude, Y., *The Finnish Dilemma*, London, 1976.

MccGwire, M., "The Rationale for Development of Soviet Sea Power," in Baylis and Segal, *Soviet Strategy*, London, 1981.

Meinander, N., *Insyn och Efterklokhet*, Helsinki, 1977.

Norsk Udenrigspolitisk Arsbok (yearly publication by Norwegian Institute for Foreign Policy, Oslo, containing articles on foreign and defense matters).

Paasikivi, J. K., *Minnen I-II*, Helsinki, 1958-59.

Palm, T., *The Finnish-Soviet Armistice Negotiations of 1944*, Stockholm, 1971.

Pokhlebkin, V. V., *Skandinavskiye Strany i SSSR*, Moscow, 1958.

SSSR-Finlandia, Moscow, 1975.

Prokofiev, V., *Severnaya Evropa i Mir*, Moscow, 1966.

Puntila, L., *The Political History of Finland 1809-1966*, London, 1975.

Skodvin, M., *Norden eller NATO*, Oslo, 1971.

Soderhjelm, I., *Tre Resor Till Moskva*, Helsinki, 1970.

Sontag, R., and I. Beddie, *Nazi-Soviet Relations 1939-41*, Washington, 1948.

Stettinius, E., *Roosevelt and the Russians: The Yalta Conference*, London, 1950.

Tanner, V., *Finlands Vag 1939-40*, Helsinki, 1950.

Vagen Till Fred 1943-44, Helsinki, 1952.

Tarulis, A., *Soviet Policy Toward the Baltic States 1918-40*, Notre Dame, 1959.

Tornudd, K., *Soviet Attitudes Towards Non-Military Regional Cooperation*, Helsinki, 1971.

Ord ock Handling, Vasa, 1982.

Tuominen, A., *Kremls Klockor*, Helsinki, 1957.

Skarans ock Hammarens Vag, Helsinki, 1958.

Udenrigsministeriet (Danish Ministry of Foreign Affairs), *Problem omkring dansk sikkerhedspolitik I-II*, Copenhagen, 1970.

Udgaard, N. M., *Great Power Politics and Norwegian Foreign Policy*, Oslo, 1973.

Ulam, A., *The Rivals: America and Russia Since World War II*, New York, 1971.

Expansion and Coexistence: Soviet Foreign Policy 1917-73, New York, 1974.

Dangerous Relations, New York, 1983.

Upton, A., *Finland in Crisis 1940-41*, London, 1964.

Communism in Scandinavia and Finland, New York, 1973.

Finland 1939-40, London, 1974.

U.S. Department of State, *Foreign Relations of the United States*, volumes concerning the Nordic area since 1946.

Utrikesdepartementet, *Utrikesfragor*, yearly publication since 1950 of official documents on Swedish foreign policy.

Vayrynen, R., *Conflicts in Finnish-Soviet Relations--Three Comparative Case Studies*, Tammersors, 1974.

Vloyantes, I., *Silk Glove Hegemony: Finnish-Soviet Relations 1944-74*, Kent, 1975.

Voronkov, L., *Severnaja Europa: Obshestvennost i problemy vuesjuej politiki*, Moscow, 1976.

Strany Severnoy Europy v Sovremennykh Mezhdunarodnykh Otnosheniakh, Moscow, 1980.

Non-Nuclear Status to Northern Europe, Moscow, 1984.

Wahlback, K., *Fran Mannerheim Till Kekkonen: Huvudlinjer i Finlandsk Politik 1917-67*, Stockholm, 1967.

Den svenska neutralitetens rotter, Stockholm, 1984.

Wheeler-Bennett, J., *et al.*, *The Semblance of Peace: The Political Settlement after World War II*, London, 1972.

Whence the Threat to Peace, 3d ed., Military Publishing House, Moscow, 1984.

Wolfe, T., *Soviet Power and Europe 1945-70*, Baltimore, 1970.

Wuorinen, I., *A History of Finland*, New York, 1965.

Finland and World War II--1939-44, New York, 1946.

Yearbook of Finnish Foreign Policy, articles by Apunen, Kommissarov, Korhonen, Ruhala, and others.